Gajanan M. Sabnis
Sharda G. Sabnis
Edward J. Martin

GREEN HOUSE
The Energy Efficient Home

Drylongso Publications
Washington, DC

Copyright © 2005 by Gajanan M. Sabnis. All Rights Reserved.

Published simultaneously in India by Vipul Prakashan, Mumbai.

No part of this publication may be reproduced, stored in retrieval system or transmitted in any form or by any means, electronic, mechanical, photocopying, recording, scanning or otherwise, except as permitted under Sections 107 or 108 of the 1976 United States Copyright Act, without either the prior written permission of the Publisher, or authorization through payment of the appropriate per-copy fee to the Copyright Clearance Center, 222 Rosewood Drive, Danvers, MA 01923, (978) 750-8400, fax (212) 750-4744. Request to the publisher for permission should be addressed the address above, or by email: drylongso.editor@drylongso.com.

This publication is designed to provide accurate and authoritative information in regard to the subject matter covered. It is sold with the understanding that the publisher is not engaged in rendering professional services or advice. If professional advice or other expert assistance is required, the services of a competent professional person should be sought.

ISBN: 0-615-12948-X.

Published by Drylongso Publications
2001 M Street, NW, Box 19795, Washington, DC 20036-9795

Dedicated To Our Parents

Shantabai and Mahadeo Sabnis
Keshar and Harishchandra Rajadhyaksha
Josephine and Edward Martin

Our parents,
who brought us in this world
and gave us all they could
to make us successful

Table of Contents

1. PREFACE — vii
2. INTRODUCTION — 1
3. FREQUENTLY ASKED QUESTIONS (FAQs) ON CONCRETE HOUSES — 19
4. ENERGY EFFICIENCY IN RESIDENTIAL CONSTRUCTION — 51
5. MATERIALS OF CONSTRUCTION — 89
6. APPLICATIONS OF CONCRETE IN HOME CONSTRUCTION — 105
7. CASE STUDIES OF ENERGY-EFFICIENT CONCRETE HOMES — 119
8. BUILDING YOUR OWN COMPOSITE CONCRETE HOME — 143
9. COMPUTER APPLICATION TO DESIGN YOUR OWN HOME — 167
10. GLOSSARY — 193

Preface

Concrete houses have been built all over the world including the United States. However, acceptance has been extremely slow for several reasons primarily because the typical homebuyer is not aware of the options available for house construction. A concrete house is usually built only when a buyer requests or demands it. Buyers often look to buy a house in a development in which construction is already underway and in which construction is usually "stick-built" or modular and of wood. The contractor or developer is conditioned to using typical construction techniques, and laborers and crafts-persons are trained in conventional methods. Retraining for applying the techniques required in concrete house construction is costly and time consuming. However, retraining attitudes of buyers, developers and contractors are the biggest stumbling blocks to wide acceptance of new types of construction.

Innovation is difficult to accept for most people; change is avoided when possible. The idea of using concrete is not radical, since it has been used in residential construction in many parts of the world, even in developing countries. There are many advantages to using concrete for house construction. In the US, buyers in states with natural hazards such as hurricanes and tornadoes should find concrete especially attractive. A concrete house will last longer than a conventionally constructed one. A typical US home buyer lives in a house for no longer than 5-10 years and therefore does not consider its long life a high priority purchase factor. Thus, the useful design life from the owner's perspective may be relatively short.

The cost of conventional materials has gone up considerably in the last two decades, while the cost of (cement) concrete has not. On the other hand, the concrete house construction techniques used today result in a slightly higher initial unit cost than conventional (in the order of a few percent). Concrete construction together with high efficiency insulation will quickly pay for the differential. The cost of energy has become high enough to make a home buyer consider the type of construction as a purchase factor.

Use of alternate materials, such as concrete and steel would also help conserve natural resources. New home construction accounts for 40 percent of the wood consumed in the United States. Although the US is home to only 5 percent of the global population, it is responsible for over 15 percent of the world's consumption of wood. A typical 1,700 square foot wood framed home requires the equivalent of clear cutting one acre of forest[1]. Last year (2004) new home starts rose to about 2 million[2], and wood frame (stick) building accounts for about 78% of all starts. The time is right therefore to look to alternate materials for housing to produce long-lasting, energy efficient and yet cost-effective homes.

A major handicap to use of concrete comes from the fact that it is perceived as being cold in winter and warm in summer. An insulated concrete house using techniques described herein will be warm in winter and cool in summer. In northern states, the use of concrete is not very well accepted, because of the home buyer's perception of concrete being a poor insulator, a "cold" and unconventional material for construction of homes. The only exception to the poor perception is the basement, where concrete is used for the floor and in walls in the form of blocks or as poured concrete.

The support of utility companies, insurers and manufacturers of alternate materials and innovative construction technology can go a long way to convince buyers and over the longer term, can enhance the value of the house. Proper education, training and suitable promotion are necessary. Several resources and publications are available on

---

[1] http://www.neo.state.ne.us//home_const/factsheets/min_use_lumber.htm
[2] http://www.neo.state.ne.us//home_const/factsheets/min_use_lumber.htm

concrete in residential home construction.[3] However, none discusses in detail the development of the house at a level suitable to educate the home buyer so that his or her questions are answered in a manner to substantially benefit from this very useful construction material in the housing industry.

This book has been mainly based on the personal experience, both good and bad, and with the motivation to make concrete a more widely used material for construction. It should serve as a guide to assist those who may consider using concrete in residential home construction. Its main purpose is to assist home buyers to change their thinking not only by having a clearer understanding of why concrete works better as a material for their home, but also to demonstrate how they can make it a better investment with lower maintenance and energy costs. It should serve as a handy reference for architects, engineers and contractors, since there is no concise and easy-to-read stylebook of its kind at the present time.

This book presents an innovative use of a composite system between concrete in various forms and recycled light-gage steel. This "total" alternative approach can be modified to use concrete and steel to varying degrees, concrete walls and conventional floors, and others. The use of wood may be totally eliminated as a structural material and its use minimized in the construction. This follows the philosophy of saving natural resources and also using a building system that is **attractive, beneficial and cost-effective** (ABC). This ABC strategy provides an entire package to the practicing architect, engineer and contractor to better understand the construction of an alternative house and to appreciate its advantages over the present available systems.

The book begins with the author's experience of designing, building and living in one such innovative and unique home. The home has a traditional external colonial appearance but with a totally different environment inside, such as the quietness and no squeaking, other noises or

---

[3] http://www.concretehomescouncil.org/b_developers/c_process.html

vibrations. Chapter One covers many "Do's and Don'ts" for the buyer. The second chapter is a key chapter in the book and consists of frequently asked questions (FAQ) by the owner and others related to concrete, energy utilization, construction techniques and many other subjects related to an energy efficient home.

Chapter Three discusses the important feature of energy efficiency, since this factor alone may take the concrete home to the next level of acceptance by the construction industry and the prospective home buyer. A discussion of alternate materials of construction follows in Chapter Four. Chapter Five considers the present use of concrete in different areas in the home. The intent is to make the reader more comfortable by understanding this type of construction, not as a new idea but one that has been and can further be used extensively.

In Chapter Six, actual case studies are presented in which concrete was used as a primary material. Chapter Seven follows with the details of designing and building a house and was the primary motivation for writing this book. It contains the author's own experience on the entire project and includes pictures with captions to indicate various stages of the project.

Chapter Eight demonstrates that the design and construction of a house is not a myth, but can be a very interesting project for an individual home buyer using the latest available computer software. The process does not have to depend totally on a custom builder's work or the efforts of an architect.

This book is based on the first author's initial idea of a concrete house and his personal experiences of four decades with various construction materials; hopefully this book demonstrates the successful use of alternate construction materials in residential construction. The other two authors, Drs. Sharda Sabnis and Edward Martin gave more ideas throughout the project and contributed immensely with their critical reviews and additional materials. In addition, Dr.

Martin, my long-term friend and former colleague at Howard University, used the concept of ICF home by building his own home in Cleveland (see Chapter Six) and hails it as an extremely successful project and "the real future home." He also wrote some of the material and did technical editing.

Finally, I must gratefully appreciate the support of my family in this venture. My wife, Sharda, in addition to participating during the construction of the house and criticizing the writing at all stages, pushed me along with our daughter, Madhavi and helped me with continuous efforts to make this book possible; our son, Rahul helped distantly from New York with the design of the cover and throughout its development with his critique. Madhavi and her friend, Jada Graves, both former graduate students in Mass Communication at Howard University provided initial assistance for editing the manuscript. I also must acknowledge the help of the Civil Engineering Class of 2004 at Howard University, as part of their individual projects in the design class; they contributed to Chapter Six and Eight with various applications and checking of the software.

Silver Spring, Maryland
Gajanan M. Sabnis
June 11, 2005

Introduction

This book is written primarily for those who believe that there is a need for change in the US housing industry to a more durable, long-lasting maintenance-free and cost-effective home. The need exists for types, single-family and multi-family units, row houses and townhouses. While housing construction has not changed a great deal in the last 50 years from stone to brick and now to wood over the last 200 years, there has not been much progress toward the use of concrete, except for the last few years. [1, 2, 3, 4] In the US, it was inevitable that the huge timber resource would lead to the dominance of wood house construction. On the other hand, the progress toward concrete in house construction in many countries without such a resource has been more prominent. This book discusses the concrete home, concrete as one of the best materials of construction, an alternate to wood that possesses substantial advantages to the homeowner in many ways, such as energy-efficiency, quietness, low maintenance and protection against many natural and man-made disasters.

Authors' Dream to Own a Home

When immigrants came to America they changed its face. In the last 40 to 50 years, South Asians including from the Indian subcontinent became a major group of immigrants to the United States and as an individual group changed it substantially, generally for the better. These immigrants came primarily for education and when they saw opportunities, they continued their life, made their careers and raised their families. These Asian immigrants mainly pursued four goals to become successful: to educate, to seek opportunity, to fulfill their lifetime professional goal and to meet social and family obligations (similar to those defined by Stephen Covey [5], an acclaimed author as four basic qualities: *"to live, to be loved, to learn, and to leave a legacy"*).

They've done well in all these areas. One of the things they dreamed, like most Americans was to own a home of their own. Obviously it takes a lot of courage for an Asian immigrant to this country to think of borrowing money to buy property with their different cultural background. So the dream of owning a house in the minds of these immigrants was somewhat of a lower priority than getting an education and seeking a career opportunity. When they had satisfied both these goals in almost two decades, it was in the early 1970's that they started fulfilling their dream of owning a home. By then many also had made the decision to live permanently in this country and accordingly, to enjoy the benefits of being an American.

My wife and I (the Sabnis's) were such immigrants and when we decided on a house; we did not have enough money to make the down payment and pay closing costs. To us, such terms as "down payment" and "closing costs" were totally foreign. We did not know much about house maintenance. In the rented apartment we lived in at the time it was easy to call the management to take care of any problems. As a homeowner, not only would we be responsible for the mortgage, but also for its maintenance. Unfortunately, when we started looking in the neighborhood that we thought we would like to live, the house prices were out of our reach. We had to wait a few more months when the financial conditions and the rules for mortgage lending changed, so that we could pay a lower down payment. We were able to buy the townhouse (Figure 1) only after waiting for six months (while a 10% increase in price occurred) until we had saved enough money for down payment. It was better than our apartment providing extra space for a little more money, and tax benefits. There was more privacy, but no garage, which we feel now that every house should have. My wife and I maintained and improved this house and lived in it for three years. When we learned more about housing and tax benefits, we bought our first single family home (Figure 2). Since it was already built and we bought it from another homeowner, we knew very little of its construction.

We lived in that house for a few years and as we continued to learn more about the housing industry, American life and becoming financially more secure, we decided to buy a new house that could serve our needs for longer period. We could watch the house being built, so that we could make necessary changes to suit our needs (Figure 3). Unfortunately, when we saw it during construction my wife was totally disappointed with the poor construction of the house. Having already made the payment, I explained to her that it was the norm for construction in this country and consoled with the idea that in the future we might build a house using our own ideas about construction. The house in Figure 3 looks pretty good from the outside, but having lived in it for seventeen years we know the energy problems it had. The construction had minimum energy standards resulting constant air leakage. The contractor tried to solve the problem with additional windowpanes, as he thought the problem was not in construction, but in the windows and other items. But for about 17 years the master bedroom was still too cold and we had to put blankets around the edges of the room so that it would be acceptably warm in winter. We finally found a solution by building the current home (Figure 4).

Figure 1. Townhouse (1974-77), our first home was 20 years old (and later became our investment property) in Silver Spring, Maryland

Figure 2. Single Family home (1977-1980), was four years old at time of purchase and was convenient to children's Barrie School, a private school in Silver Spring, Maryland

Figure 3. Single family home (1980-97) built by a commercial developer as a new home with conventional materials. It was convenient to children's school until they graduated to go to college; also in Silver Spring, Maryland.

Figure 4. Present energy-efficient home (1997- present), with a new concept and the main source of research and experience for this book

Dream Becomes a Reality

From the engineering or an architectural perspective, the problem in our old house was air leakage through the siding and around the windows, which could not be mitigated by adding extra conventional fiberglass insulation, given the type of construction used. The leaks would still allow the air to enter usually where it was most undesirable. The house was not small for the family, but too small to have large social gatherings and classical music programs, which we enjoyed. In the early 1990's, we purchased land for a custom-built house with our own design. I was motivated with the presentation on the *"House of the Future"* in 1995 at the Pre-cast/Pre-stressed Concrete Institute (PCI) in a Marketing Council meeting. The presentation was about concrete houses in this country and how the concrete industry had a very small share of the housing market. The speaker's biggest point was the large size of the US residential home industry - of the order of $125 billion (in 1995).

The speaker was "preaching to the choir" of engineers and not homeowners, who may be potentially interested in building concrete houses. It just happened that my wife and I had the plans ready and wanted to use his idea to experiment with this new alternate material as well as to increase the share of concrete in residential construction. Although the idea was good for my "entrepreneurial mind," my wife was totally opposed to it, having lived in a house that was cold in winter. She had perceived the concrete house to be cold in winter and warm in summer. After several arguments (and since we were planning to build a house anyway), she reluctantly agreed to give me a chance to build a concrete house, as long as her conditions were fulfilled. They were easy enough to meet and after staying in this comfortable house, she is so happy that she does not want to move out for a long time to come. Figure 4 shows the house after seven years. The rest of this book is devoted to various aspects of concrete house construction, energy efficiency and some other direct and indirect benefits of the concrete home. Much of the commentary is based, on first hand knowledge.

A Short History of Concrete in Residential Homes

Since it has been known to be a construction material, concrete has been used in residential applications for a long time. Certain parts of a house need concrete in one form or another. In the basement, use of concrete is inevitable either as poured-in material or as block masonry, and these uses have a long history. As part of the basement wall, footings were always in concrete as the only material suitable and proper for its use. Moving to the level above the basement, the use of concrete has been almost non-existent. As an early example, one can cite Frank Lloyd Wright's house (1939), but that house is a very special application and cannot be considered as a general use of concrete in residential homes. Using concrete in residential construction did not gain attention until the 1970's and as of 2004 not much progress has been made. Organizations such as The Portland Cement Association (PCA), the National Association of Home Builders (NAHB) and others, including the Insulated Concrete Forms Association (ICFA), have been in the forefront of this development. PCA demonstrates the favorable use of concrete and projects in future residential applications[4].

Present Practice

As mentioned earlier, the practice of using concrete in construction as blocks or even with stone or brick remained steady for years. In the late 1960's, attempts were made during the Nixon administration by the Department of Housing and Urban Development (HUD), to make innovations in residential concrete by challenging the construction industry

---

[4]http://www.concretehomescouncil.org/b_developers/c_process.html

through a program called "Operation Breakthrough."[5] A system was developed by the author at the American Cement Corporation (ACC) to include the use of cement in the form of panelized construction of homes, with stucco on the outside and a core of hexagonal cells of heavy-duty Kraft paper and gypsum board on the inside. [6] Due to the lack of follow-up of these schemes on both sides, government as well as the private industry, things did not change much until there was a need developed in the late 1970's, when inflation resulted in a much higher increase in construction material costs, particularly in wood compared to cement and concrete.

Due to the oil embargo in the 1970's and energy "crises," more attention was paid to other materials of construction, better insulation and construction techniques. The use of insulated concrete forms made concrete more viable in residential construction. In the 1990's, the Portland Cement Institute (PCI) made great strides in constructing buildings using pre-cast concrete panels for concrete work, but again with only limited success in residential construction. This lack of progress during the period was mainly attributed to the perceived need for heavy equipment for residential concrete construction. The need for heavy equipment made residential construction more expensive than conventional – wood - building systems.

Current Practice - Year 2000 and Present

Since the late 1990's until the present there has been a mild surge of activity in the use of concrete in residential house construction. The PCA, NAHB, ICFA, US Department of Housing and Urban Development (HUD) provide with Websites and available information on the topic (list at the end of the chapter). In most instances, the external walls in residential construction have been changed to include insulated concrete forms (ICF), but floors have remained

---

[5]http://archives.gov/research_room/federal_records_guide/general_department_of_housing_and urban_rg207.html (*see 207.7.2 Records of the Office of Public Affairs*)

conventionally constructed of wood. Due to the convenience of using materials consistently, the emphasis should not only be placed on the concrete walls in ICF, but also on the other elements of the house to result in a total system that is unique and easy to build. The concept is not new and it is convincingly simple and comprehensible to architects, engineers, developers and even to the owner, if given chance to choose alternate and better system.

The Future of Concrete Homes

The availability of computers and the wide variety of design software allow the owners to develop their own design, with the help of knowledgeable professionals. Similarly, housing developers could use computer-aided design to expose contractors and potential home buyers to the choice for building materials and the advantages to be gained from building and living in concrete houses. Housing developments can be made unique thereby attracting more home buyers. Some of the non-construction benefits are quietness, fire-resistance, protection from termites and importantly, non-squeaking structures, especially floors and staircases. Promotional emphasis on these and other advantages will make concrete industry efforts more successful in the coming decade and lead to a significant share of residential applications.

The homebuilder shows in locations, such Dallas and Las Vegas, annually draw hundreds of thousands of attendees. Promotions at these and other shows around the U.S. demonstrate that homes built in a short period of a few days (albeit after months of off-site preparation), but attendees generally leave with the idea that these are special, custom-built, expensive homes not for the typical homeowner. Discussions with many in the industry have demonstrated that the resources may be spent wisely through such information dissemination channels and result in the education of large numbers of people. The typical American family with computer-savvy children and parents watches movies without realizing that substantial scenes are computer-generated depictions of events and effects use animation and simulation. Commercially available computer software can be used in home design, which could help promote the growth of new concepts in the construction industry, especially for concrete home construction.

Award-winning Concrete/Energy-Efficient Home

The main theme of this book relates to a traditional looking home, but uses an entirely new concept of materials and systems to make attractive, yet maintenance-free homes that will last for generations. ICFs wrap the walls the entire height of the house; use of recycled light-gauge steel and concrete provide stable high strength floors; finally, the use of geothermal energy reduces substantially the energy cost of conventional electrical, gas or oil for both heating and cooling. The National Capital Chapter of the American Concrete Institute (ACI) presented the house shown in Figure 4 with an award for innovative use of concrete. Articles about our award-winning home were published in national society journals and through international presentations around the globe. [4, 7, 8]

U.S. Practice vs. Global Practice

The authors have observed through experiences of either living or working both in the underdeveloped and developed countries and through worldwide travel that every country has its own construction practice. Using ideas from all over the world provides a sound base for making progress. In the US and Canada, residential homes are typically made of conventional wood construction, while in the rest of the world, alternate materials, such as concrete other materials are commonly used. As the world has shrunk due to the rapid growth in communications and travel, technology transfer will increasingly see that we all benefit from innovations and efficiency in the construction industry. Concrete and concrete related materials were used in the world much before America was discovered. It is only a matter of time until these materials will become common globally.

Energy Efficiency

More emphasis has been placed on the use of concrete for energy efficiency but the progress is very slow in changing the perception of concrete not being a very friendly material due to its 'cold' appearance. Concrete retains heat by its very nature because of its high thermal mass. When cement is mixed with water the reaction is exothermic releasing heat, which makes it a good material to pour in most areas and in most weather conditions (although not below a certain temperature) particularly with insulated forms. High thermal mass allows the concrete to be more energy-efficient than conventional materials.

Energy efficiency of materials can be compared using three different parameters: R-value, passage of air and thermal mass. Comparison (Table 1) [2] indicates that concrete with insulated forms (ICF) is twice as effective not only for R-value, but also for air infiltration. Concrete walls used as an outside envelope along with proper floors and connections make a house very "tight," resisting air infiltration. Proper ventilation maintains indoor air quality. Experience says that tightness does not pose a problem. An air exchanger can provide sufficient ventilation in an ICF home. These three aspects put together will result in as much as 25-30 per cent energy savings, thus benefiting the owner directly by lower expenses per month.

Energy efficiency can be further enhanced by the use of additional forms of alternate energy, such as solar or geothermal. These aspects will be found later including comparison between various materials of construction and their efficiencies in terms of utility costs.

Table 1. Energy Performance Data for Alternate Wall Systems (adapted from Ref. 2)

Property	Measure	Typical value for wall of:		
		ICF	2x4	2x6
Resistance to conduction	R	18-35	10-12	15-19
Air Infiltration	ACH^1 (for house)	0.1-0.35	0.3-0.7*	0.3-0.7*
Resistance to conduction	R	15-35	10-12	15-19

*Air infiltration does not generally indicate much difference in two walls
^{1}Air changes per hour

Energy efficiency can be further enhanced by the use of additional forms of alternate energy, such as solar or geothermal, both the gifts of Mother Nature to the mankind. More on these aspects will be found later including comparison between various construction materials and their efficiencies in terms of utility costs.

Government vs. Private Role in Energy-Efficient Construction

Government at the federal, state and county levels has taken the initiative to promote the concept; this has been done largely on a voluntary basis. Mandatory requirements and long term financial and tax incentives for energy saving and the use of newer construction technologies would accelerate widespread use of concrete and other alternate materials.

On the private sector side, there has to be united front, using a "win-win-win" approach. These three "wins" refer to education, training and demonstrating. The goal should not be "promoting concrete" directly, but utilizing its advantages to benefit the home-owner. Education comes from the private sector and public universities and in part, with support from government agencies. Some financial initiatives exist for the use of concrete, but more and permanent ones need to be followed by changing the strategy. Publications and meetings with others within the industry will not go too far. Training of individuals who are looking for a change and some new ideas to work in their careers is required. Demonstration projects at exhibitions or home shows will be useful if not projecting the image of building exclusive and expensive homes. Energy incentives tried by some utility companies are excellent and should be pursued.

"Best" House - Teamwork: Different Perspectives

If progress is to be made in house construction innovation, the professionals involved in the industry must recognize the importance of change. It is important not to identify the concrete house as a specialty house, which suggests higher cost and architectural uniqueness, but to make the average (prospective) homeowner aware of the real benefits which come with such a house. To make a successful change, a partnership is required among the technical professionals, contractors, developers, and potential buyers and builders.

In our case, we were the prospective owners of the house and thought about a concrete house first. Although our family had some reservations on its viability, we demonstrated an entrepreneurial attitude and made the idea work with our own resources. We talked to an architect for its development. In spite of being Professional Engineers, we still chose other structural engineers for the sake of having an engineer on record. In addition, we needed a contractor to build the house with our input. We then tried subsequently to educate the public and promote the idea to get individuals interested in the energy efficiency, concrete or other construction materials and innovative homes, who could pursue an economic and useful future project of a similar nature. This book has such a vision.

The Owner's Viewpoint

The prospective owner makes a decision either to buy a house from a developer or another homeowner, or to build one. How should he/she approach this housing project that is likely to be the largest investment of his/her lifetime and still enjoy the experience of living in it? Therefore, an owner takes a substantial risk by investing resources to build and own the house whether financing with cash or borrowing money.

One of the choices would be to go to a real estate agent and use his/her services for buying a house, which eventually must be paid for. It's the buyer that finally gets "stuck" with the house and perhaps after the initial period of one year with warranty etc., the homeowner becomes responsible for its maintenance no matter what happened during the previous ownership. Basically, a house needs to be maintained until the time of a subsequent sale.

The second choice is that a prospective buyer may go to a new development looking for a new house and may be impressed with externalities by touring the new model. This model is probably built the same way as any house in the development would be, but more importantly it is furnished well to attract him and his family. In this case, for the developer to insure that the house is sold at the asking price there may be hardly any price negotiation. Many things shown in the model are extras and are added on, and one has to carefully ask questions and evaluate the extra costs. As a general rule, it is easy to pay for these add-ons in the beginning by financing them through the mortgage with relatively small increases in monthly payments.

The third choice is involving an additional step of buying an individual lot and then building a custom-built home. This choice requires recognition of the problems associated with engaging a contractor and evaluating progress, or subcontracting and supervising the activities and progress or each subcontractor personally. Regardless of the choice made, the owner should be aware of the pros and cons of each type of house construction. Concrete houses can offer advantages and disadvantages as shown on the Table 2 below.

Table 2. Favorable Factors for Concrete Houses

Factor	Comment
Resistance to Severe Storm Damage	High
Energy Efficiency	High, Using the ICF Technique
External Noise Attenuation	High
Internal Noise Attenuation	High, Using Hybrid Composite Floors
Maintenance	Low, Depending on External Surface Finish
Durability – Life	Long
Internal Space – Space Utilization	Long Spans Possible With Composite Floors
Capital Cost	Small Percentage; Higher Initial Cost
Maintenance Cost	Low, Depending on External Surface Finish

Civil or structural engineer hardly plays a role in residential construction in the U.S. As an engineer I also believe we have an obligation to make an impact on residential designs. When the architects design or make an aesthetic plan for an owner, the responsibility still falls on an engineer to design it properly so it becomes a safe structure for the occupant or the owner. This safety can be given only by means of proper design and taking into account proper materials. In the case of residential homes after the plans are prepared, the engineering work in general is traditionally done without an engineers help. Although an architect is legally allowed to submit the drawings to get the approval from the county or the local authorities to build the house, the contractor who gives the bid to the architect or the owner goes ahead with his business of constructing it. Thus, looking at various elements in the residential structure, the engineer is rarely involved because traditionally he has not been an active team player.

An Architect's Perspective

The architect is an important player of a successful energy efficient home. Thus if somebody talks about a successful residential project the first profession to take credit or be given credit by the public at large would be an architect.

An architect's role in housing is important because he/she has been trained to look at a product, from the point of view of appeal to the owner. The owner will therefore approach an architect to find out how a house may be built and the architect will assume an important role of being a responsible link between the owner and the contractor. The architect will work out a set of drawings with typical sections and details so they can be submitted to the local housing authorities for the building permit(s). It is important therefore, that the architect be aware of the potential for high-strength, energy efficient options for home construction.

Contractor/Developer's Perspective

Another player on the team who helps in accomplishing a successful project is the contractor or the developer. From the contractor's/developer's perspective, the project will move forward only if either of them have something to invest for the success of the project and are in it as partners. From the developer's perspective, it is not very difficult to construct a house in an alternate manner, since the design has been made and craftsperson will perform the construction. On the other hand, the owner has something to gain by making a commitment to live in the house, which he or his family can enjoy and the developer or the contractor who have a stake in the project can expect to recover a substantial return.

Our present house was designed and put out for a bid for both conventional and alternate construction materials (although there was an initial resistance because of the alternate materials). The bid from the contractor on a conventional basis was 5% lower than for alternate materials and techniques. A few percent higher for alternate concrete construction has been the experience elsewhere as well.

Another point to be made here is that in any new type of construction, there are initial obstacles to be overcome, including the need to change the way of thinking. As an example, when the foundation is built concrete is usually used in conventional wood construction practice. On the other hand, the construction of the basement wall using insulated concrete forms (ICF) is straightforward to assemble and the ICFs act as formwork during construction. In recent years, concrete construction has become easier because the contractors have begun to accept concrete as a construction material and not necessarily as a heavy non-friendly material.

References

1. VanderWerf, P.A. and Munsell, W. K., *"Concrete Homebuilding Systems"*, McGraw Hill, New York, NY. 1994

2. VanderWerf, P.A. et al, *"Insulating Concrete Forms"*, McGraw Hill, New York, NY. 1997

3. Sabnis G.M. and Sabnis, S.G., *"Hybrid Energy Efficient Home"*, Concrete International, Published by American Concrete Institute (ACI), July 2000

4. Conner, H.W., *"Residential Concrete"*, National Home Builders' Association (NAHB), Washington, DC, 1997.

5. Covey, S.R et al, *"First Things First: To Live, to Love, to Learn, to Leave a Legacy"*, Franklin Covey Press, New York, 1994

6. Sabnis, G.M. and Aroni, S., *"Use of Paper Honeycomb Panels in Housing Construction"*, Panelized Structural Assemblies, Montreal, Canada, May 1972

7. Sabnis, G.M., *"Energy-efficient Dream Concrete Home: A Reality"*, Educational Seminar presented in Edison, NJ, April 2004

8. Sabnis G.M. and Sabnis, S.G., *"Building an Energy Efficient Home"*, Proceedings of the International Conference of ASCE India Section, September 1998.

Websites with General Information

http://www.cement.org/

GREEN HOUSE: THE ENERGY EFFICIENT HOME

Site for various Portland Cement Documents
http://www.forms.org
Site for documents published by the Insulated Concrete Forms Association
http://www.nahb.org/
Site for publications by National Association of Home Builders

Frequently Asked Questions (FAQs) on Concrete Houses

Purpose of This Chapter

The purpose of this chapter is to present the most frequently asked questions by anyone who wants to build an energy-efficient house; concrete happens to be one of the recent construction materials that has contributed toward the goal of energy efficiency. The concrete house is by far the most durable, maintenance-free house with many desirable characteristics. The questions in this chapter have come from various sources including engineers, architects and others in the building profession, and lay persons who want to build such homes.

When this book was conceived there were many questions unanswered. Such questions are often referred to as frequently asked questions (FAQs) and should be answered to one's own satisfaction when thinking about using concrete and the energy-efficient home. We, as the prospective home owners needed answers before proceeding with the project of building our own homes. The Sabnis house finally became an enviable product and won awards and acclamation.

The questions and answers should help the reader to identify portions of the book for further reading and to formulate an idea of a project that could be undertaken. On one hand, the questions begin as a simple one: why build your own house rather that buying one from a builder or a developer? On the other hand, these basic questions may arise out of different aspects of the house related to the site, materials of construction (mainly concrete), energy-efficiency (which has been the most important issue to many even as of this day) and finally the cost. A simple question may have multiple answers depending on different perspectives.

They are arranged in several groups for ease in referring to them. These groups are:
a. General interest;
b. Planning (including energy and efficiency);
c. Design (including materials);
d. Construction;
e. Other (including esthetics).

General Interest FAQs

How big is the market for housing in the U.S.?

There are various estimates; the most recent statistic shows that the industry in single family and row houses (predominantly called residential), and excluding the multi-story housing, is in the order $150 billion.

What part of the housing market can the concrete industry or the alternate materials of construction realistically have?

Certain house components have always been made with concrete or with cement-related materials—for example, foundation, basement slabs, patio, garage floor, driveway, and steps have typically been made of concrete. Concrete home construction has occupied perhaps 5% of the market at the most. Of the total market value, some parts will be non-structural or non-construction material type such as carpeting, finishing and the appliances which may add up to as much as 30%. Of the remaining 65% (about $100 million), concrete may expect some significant share along with other alternate materials.

Why a concrete house?

There is really no answer, or many answers, to this question. Houses have been built mainly in wood for generations; earlier, houses were constructed in stone and later in brick and they served well. Wooden houses became more and more common because of the availability of wood. But timber is becoming an increasingly scarce resource. Thus, concrete provides a good alternate material for construction.

Concrete houses are built all over the world, so what is different about them in the US?
Concrete houses are built in many countries including in many developing countries, where wood is not available for construction. However, in those countries concrete is used in a somewhat inefficient manner. Concrete is sometimes used for columns and beams and then brick walls may be added which are rarely needed for structural or aesthetic purposes. The idea of concrete houses in this country is to use the concrete for the walls as an energy storage material due to its mass. A typical façade which could be either brick or vinyl or even stucco is then added to the wall surfaces. However, stucco is a more a contemporary material and is not as prevalent in the Northeast US as in other parts.

Does a concrete home have an appeal to the general public only to engineers or architects who can appreciate them?
The general public needs to know the advantages of a concrete home and is slowly coming to do so. Rarely does the home buyer look at the house during its construction. Also, a house is often sold from owner to owner or by the developer or a builder to the homeowner, in which case the seller/developer pretty much controls what the buyer sees. In the case of a development sale amenities are added for viewing in an attractive model home. If a typical home buyer goes to a development and sees a model home, the home he/she will buy does not include the amenities shown in the model house. Few will take the opportunity to study the construction techniques apparent at houses underway in the development.

Are concrete homes built by individual owners only or can they be built as a development?
Discussions with several contractors reveal that, at this time concrete houses are built only at the request of the

customer. There is no reason why they cannot be built in a community if indeed the idea becomes popular, in which case both the developer and the owner can benefit. In a few years the concept will become popular because the advantages will be better known.

Should the concrete house be considered an energy efficient home?

Yes. A common perception of concrete is that it's cold in winter and warm in summer. This perception is not correct since the concrete mass can be used to advantage for heat retention and ultimately energy saving. Energy efficiency comes from two factors: if the outside walls of the concrete house are made energy efficient, their thermal capacity is better than the conventional wood home. Compared to a conventional R-value of 19, a properly insulated concrete house could have a value of $R = 30$, making it more efficient in terms of heating in winter or cooling in summer. The other form of energy cost saving may come from the use of geothermal or solar energy to increase efficiency further.

Will the concrete house be difficult to finish and will it look different than the conventional one?

The concrete house can be finished exactly like the conventional home. After construction, one could hardly differentiate between the conventional and the new energy efficient home except for its advantages. Often, when one buys a home, the construction material is not known.

Will it take longer to build a concrete home compared to a conventional home?

No, it will not. In fact, newer technology provides that the house in concrete can be prefabricated like wooden prefabricated homes.

Will the concrete floor be very heavy in a concrete home?

A concrete floor can be heavy if it is built in concrete alone; if it is built as a composite concrete/metal floor, it will not be much heavier than a conventional wood floor. The composite floor is lighter than concrete alone because the metal and concrete each bear part of the load. The concrete floor will be very sturdy and may be finished conventionally with hardwood or tiles. The typical conventional floor is quite thin and besides transmitting the sound, it will usually squeak eventually.

Does a concrete home have any disadvantages for the telephone system?

Concrete and steel may reduce signals for cell phones. However, current cell phone technology is not affected. Conventional phone systems are not affected.

What about saving in homeowner's insurance cost?

Insurance companies will consider concrete a safer and better construction material compared to conventional wood. Many insurance companies will consider the home built in concrete as a stone house for a better insurance rate. A potential buyer should check locally and with the insurance company.

How does concrete help with regard to insects and termites, which are often a problem?

A concrete house will provide better protection against such natural problems. Except for utility openings, insects find it more difficult to enter the concrete house with both walls and floors of concrete. Termites have virtually no venue. In addition, the house will provide better dust protection. Experience shows that there is less intrusion of dust compared to the conventional house.

Is concrete considered a non-conventional material for residential construction?

No. Concrete houses have been built in the US in a higher price range as custom homes. Presently, quality concrete can be used as an alternate material for residential construction with only small differences in cost. Concrete is used in multi-story buildings for floors as pre-cast concrete planks, but in single family homes cast in place concrete is rare.

If I want to build a concrete house, how do I go about it?

You are the homeowner and you are going to pay for everything that goes inside the house and therefore you are the one who generally will control how your house should be built, what materials should be used and so on. Although at this point there are not many contractors who will undertake the concrete home building job, the number is increasing. Organizations such as the Insulated Concrete Form Association (ICFA) have interest in the formwork of concrete, which becomes an integral part of the concrete systems. Also the Portland Cement Association (PCA), National Association of Home Builders Research Center (NAHBRC), and the Department of Energy (DOE) have substantial available literature which one can refer to through their websites. A list of references is provided at the end of the book. These will provide you with all the information related to concrete construction.

If I build a concrete home, how difficult will it be to resell?

Not difficult at all. In fact, it should be an advantage for a seller (and the buyer) when the advantages are considered.

Why are there not too many concrete homes around?

Perhaps because either the public has not demanded information or people have not been made aware of all advantages of a concrete home. Wooden homes have been built for generations and will continue to be built; therefore concrete homes will not dominate the residential market for many years. However, as time goes by and more information becomes available to the homeowner there will be a greater demand for housing with better quality, less maintenance and higher energy efficiency.

Why would a utility company be interested to have energy efficiency when they can sell more energy and make money?
The utility company wants to provide energy for more homes. They can achieve this with more energy efficient homes. This provides an incentive and encouragement to the company to promote program to analyze homes for efficiency and even give a subsidy to individual homes for the extra cost involved in making a home energy efficient or using an energy efficient system.

What alternate energy systems are available to help reduce energy cost?
There are several alternate systems compared to the conventional system of energy that we receive from the local utility companies. The most popular ones are solar and wind systems, which may not be efficient in many parts of the country. Solar panels are economical at only a small scale and largely applicable in sunlight dominated areas. Windmills can develop energy on a small-scale basis for residential purposes. A third available system is called geothermal that uses heat from the earth.

What is geothermal energy?
Geothermal energy uses heat in the earth below the frost line, where the temperature is typically at 58°F year round. Water at this temperature may be used for heating and cooling the house. In summer the warm water is taken below, cooled and brought back up; heat is exchanged in a heat exchanger. In winter, on the other hand, the house needs to be heated from 58°F to say, 70°F while the ambient temperature is 15°-25°F. So, auxiliary heating may be required for only a percentage of the time to make up the temperature differential.

Does the concrete house look any different than the conventional home?

The house can be finished as per the owner's choice of aesthetics and will be very traditional looking. In some parts of the US, the houses are more popular in a contemporary finished look such as stucco or even Spanish style, but in the northeast, they are more conservative where people prefer colonial style homes. All styles can be constructed in concrete.

Where can I get information on building a concrete home?

A good place to start is the web site: http://www.concretehomes.com of the Portland Cement Association. The PCA produces a newsletter available by email, sources of technical support, show homes, home plans, information on sizing HVAC, and other items of interest.

What is the difference between cement and concrete?

Cement is the gray powder that acts as a binder for the aggregates to make concrete. Another way to say it is "Cement is to concrete as flour is to bread". In other words one could not make a sandwich out of flour or could not make a driveway out of cement. Cement combines with water to form a stone-like mass. When the paste (cement & water) is added to aggregates (sand & gravel or stone) it acts as an adhesive and binds the aggregates together to form concrete.

What other qualities of concrete houses can we depend on?

Many indirect benefits of a concrete house built with insulating concrete forms (ICFs) exist for only slightly additional cost of the ordinary wood frame. ICF's are simple to assemble, consolidate several construction steps into one and can be economical even with the use of higher quality materials of construction. Fire resistance, less noise and wind resistance are just a few other benefits.

How much does an ICF house cost?

Houses built with ICF cost no more than 3-5% more than wood frame houses of the same design. Typically, new US homes cost $60-100 per square foot excluding land cost depending on the location. ICF walls add another $1.00-$4.00 to it. Savings in energy cost and the use of smaller heating and cooling equipment can cut the cost of the final house by an estimated $0.75 per square foot. So the net extra cost will range from $0.25 to $3.25 per square foot.

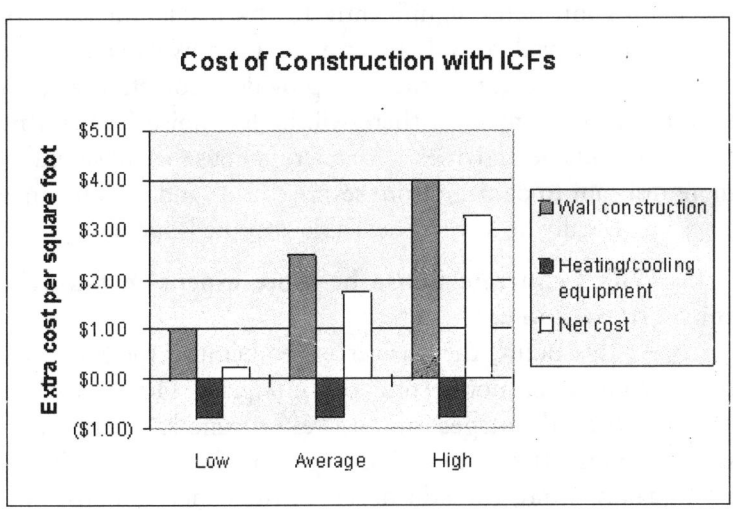

Planning *(including energy and efficiency)*

What other materials can be used in building a house?

Besides wood, concrete, stone, brick, even steel have come into the picture in the last twenty years. Steel, like concrete, is a man-made material and has worked out quite well. The steel industry has expended considerable effort to make steel houses popular, but just like concrete, steel houses have not become widely accepted. Steel has been generally used in multi-story and residential buildings, but in single-family homes, wood is still the most common material even though wood has become increasingly imported for house construction.

What are the advantages of a concrete home compared to the conventional home?
There are a number of advantages of a concrete home. It is likely that concrete houses will have a higher resale value. In the case of a concrete home, the outer wall is typically concrete poured in foam forms, which means in addition to using the mass of concrete for heat retention and insulation the foam contributes significantly to the insulation value of the composite wall, as well as acting as a formwork during the construction. The composite wall provides protection against sound transmission; thus, there will be less noise from traffic and other outside activities. A concrete house is considerably more resistant to damage from severe storms and maintenance costs will usually be lower. See Table 2 in the last chapter.

Will a concrete house be more expensive than the conventional home?
At this point, the answer is yes because the idea of a concrete house has not become commonplace. However when it does, the advantages of cost effectiveness, energy cost savings plus the protection against hazards such as earthquakes, wind, tornado or snow, the concrete house will certainly stand.

What about electrical and other utility outlets?
During the planning stage of the house, outlets and conduits are provided as a part of the wall exactly in the same way as in conventional construction. The thermal insulation provided by the foam formwork is quite thick (about 2 inches) and this thickness can be used to provide for conduits and outlets without penetrating the concrete.

Can one buy concrete to use in the house similar to timber or wood at hardware store or a lumberyard?
No. Concrete typically comes from a ready-mix plant and is delivered to the site in a concrete truck. One needs to

calculate the quantity of concrete needed and then order it accordingly. The concrete will be typically 3,000-4,000 psi strength and is generally pumped easily. Wooden walls are built by 2-3 people. The concrete wall with insulated concrete forms is built with a small crew also.

How does the cost compare between wood and concrete as construction materials?

Wood was definitely a cheaper material of construction perhaps 25 or 30 years ago even though concrete was not costly. However, in the last 10-25 years, wood prices have risen sharply compared to concrete. Concrete may have gone up about 20% while other construction materials such as wood or steel have gone up about 100%.[6]

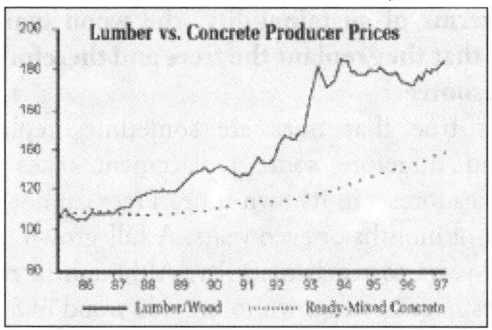

What other materials does one need in building a concrete home?

Concrete as such cannot be used by itself in all applications. Concrete is strong in compression but less strong in tension and therefore it needs reinforcement whenever it is likely to be required to bear tension loads. Reinforcement is generally provided using steel. Often polypropylene fibers are used as an additive to protect concrete from cracking, which may happen due to improper curing. These fibers are very fine and they're distributed evenly during the mixing of the concrete and are not generally visible.

---

[6] http://www.forms.org/product_info/product_benefits.html

We have heard the word sustainability these days, what does that mean in terms of a concrete house?
Sustainability means many things to many people. A simple definition of sustainability is to preserve natural resources and environmental quality for our future generations. One of the major advantages of concrete is that we are not using natural resources like wood. For most houses one has to cut trees (indeed that is inevitable), but data show that many trees are saved by building a house without wood. For a typical house of about 2,500-3,000 ft^2, one saves as many as 40-60 trees depending on the extent of use of wood; avoiding wood construction results in a substantial saving of natural resources.

In terms of sustainability, the wood manufacturers also claim that they replant the trees and therefore replenish nature's resources?
It is true that trees are sometimes replanted after cutting and therefore some replacement takes place, but nature makes forests in its own time. Trees cannot grow again in a matter of months or even years. A full-grown tree takes as long as 30 years to reach maturity. Although in recent times hybrid trees have been grown to provide wood in 5 to10 years, the quality of this wood may be inferior.

How difficult is it to build a concrete home and to obtain the permits to build it?
Generally speaking there is no problem. However, problems may occur if the building inspector or the permit officer is not familiar with the construction technique initially. Although construction drawings of buildings are often prepared and signed by an engineer or architect for structural safety reasons, often this is not the case for residential homes. Delays can be avoided by education.

How did the idea of an energy efficient concrete home come about?

The idea of a concrete home (although not new) was restricted to a few select expensive homes; however some ten years ago the marketing committees of the associations related to cement and concrete, mainly the Portland Cement Association (PCA) and Pre-stress Concrete Institute (PCI) discussed the idea and found out that a very small portion of the residential housing industry was occupied by concrete. In 1995, the total residential construction industry was of the order of $125 billion of which less than 5% was related to concrete. This was mainly in the basement walls (in the form of concrete blocks or poured concrete), the footings for these walls, some steps and the patio. The remainder of the home was mainly wood. In the last 10 years that percentage increased from 5% to about 10%, but there is a long way to go before a reasonable market share is captured. It will take some aggressive marketing by the organizations such as PCA, ACI and the National Association of Home Builders (NAHB) to promote concrete in residential use.

What is an "experienced contractor"?

An experienced contractor is the one who has built at least one concrete home and understands the principles of concrete construction well. As with any innovative construction technique, the more the crew works with insulated concrete forms (ICF), the more efficient it will be in putting them together. ICF wall-building crews report that costs drop sharply after building just 4 or 5 houses. They continue to realize savings with continued experience, but at a slower rate. The chart here is shown as a qualitative one as of 1999, but it should help understand the gains. Contractors also need experience to size the heating and cooling equipment correctly. Heating and cooling contractors not experienced with homes as energy-efficient as ICF houses should install equipment sized properly for a house using manufacturers' recommendations. These are commercial manufacturers and will help with the design of such equipment and help the owner with potential savings. Experienced contractors also size the equipment more accurately. The chart is from the web site of the Insulated Concrete Forms Association.[7]

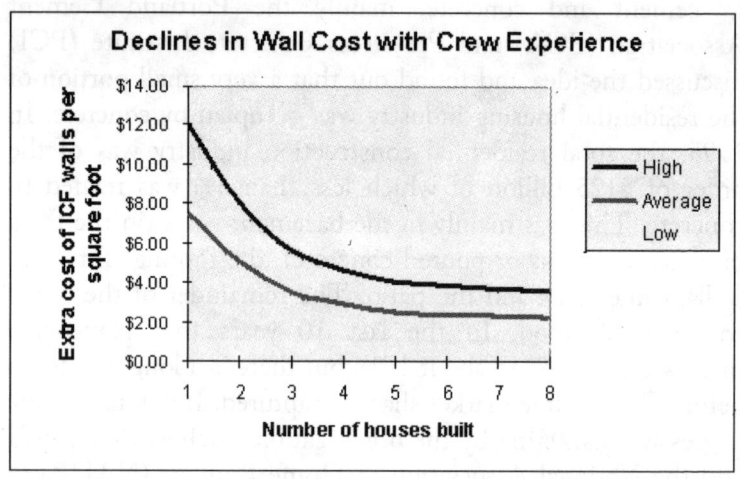

What is an energy efficient home?

Until relatively recently, energy conservation was not a design and construction criterion. In the last 30 years, the need to conserve energy has been recognized. In the 1970's, with an "energy crisis" and moratoria on building new homes, serious attempts were begun to achieve energy efficiency. Two considerations have resulted, attention to alternate sources of energy, and preventing leakage of heat energy into or out of house and other structures. Electrical appliances have been made more energy efficient and the house can be made more energy efficient by not losing it through many sources of leakage, such as walls, roof and windows. This is done more easily with a concrete home.

---

[7] http://www.forms.org/product_info/product_benefits.html

Can energy efficiency be achieved by using conventional materials?

Yes. Instead of using a conventional wooden frame, a conventional frame with thicker outside walls or a stone or a brick house can be built to achieve energy efficiency. Energy transfer reduction can be achieved by installing one of the many insulation types available to achieve virtually any R-value desired. Energy lost through the windows and window frames can be reduced by selecting one of the many energy-saving window types available for new or replacement applications.

Does the energy efficient home cost a lot more?

Energy efficient home does cost more, but it also repays back in a short period during the life of the house. Cost increase depends on the type of system, size of the house and on location. If one combines the different material systems and the energy resources for energy efficiency, this higher cost of approximately between 5-10%, which can be repaid in terms of saving of the energy cost in less than 10 years on a monthly basis. The house will also be very well maintenance-free.

Energy efficient (concrete) home seems quite appealing and attractive. Have the government and the private sector done to help you or help get into new types of construction?

Change is inevitable, but it is very difficult to achieve in a short time. The federal government in fact looked into alternate construction materials in the late 1960's and launched the program called "Operation Breakthrough," during the time George Romney was the Secretary of Housing, Urban and Development. It was not successful. There are a number of programs in existence today, which are described in detail in other chapters of this book. The Department of Energy (DOE), Environmental Protection Agency (EPA) as well as Department of Housing, Urban and

Development (HUD) have active programs including some research work conducted with National Science Foundation (NSF). In the private sector, the steel industry has promoted their steel structures to replace wood, which is perhaps easier to do then replacing the wood with concrete. The concrete industry for a long time has been happy with the use of concrete in residential construction in the foundation or as concrete blocks or as retaining walls in the basement. Insulated concrete forms (ICF) came into existence in the early 90's, and since then organizations such as Portland Cement Association (PCA), National Ready Mix Concrete Association (NRMCA) and the statewide ready mix concrete associations have active in promoting concrete houses.

What are the main hurdles in making use of alternate construction materials, such as concrete to build energy efficient homes?

Building a home is a team effort and in doing so various groups of individuals and trades must come together to work. The players in this team include the owner, the architect and/or engineer, tradespersons, the county inspector(s) for approval and finally the contractor to build it. Some of these elements may be pulled together by the developer. The owner may take the lead, but may need some education related to construction. No matter how good the project is conceptually it nevertheless will need the support from the buyer for its acceptance. Therefore, the biggest concern at this point is education.

Which is the biggest stumbling block for making use of this system?

The biggest stumbling block will be development of expertise of the contractor/developer and awareness on the part of the homeowner to insist on alternate choices.

Since the different materials come from their manufacturers, what efforts are being made by them to support the user?

In today's time, with computer technology, most manufacturers provide such information on their websites and are very helpful with the technical support for the user. They also have associations, which try to help the industry by quality products by these manufacturers. They also provide education and research background information to make these products safe. Examples are given throughout is answers to questions.

We hear a number, the "R-value" for energy use or energy efficiency. What is it?

"R-value" signifies the ability of a material to resist heat flow. The higher the R-value, the greater is the heat flow resistance. For instance, it's more difficult for heat to pass through R-20 insulation than it is to pass through R-10 insulation. Some materials are naturally better insulators than others. For example, a six-inch batt of fiberglass insulation has an R-value of 19, while an eight-inch concrete block has an R-value of 1.04. Glass, like concrete block, also has little resistance to heat—a single pane of glass has an R-value of 1.13.

How much will I save in an energy-efficient home?

Houses built with ICF exterior walls require an estimated 40% less energy to heat and 30% less energy to cool than comparable frame houses. A typical 2,000 square foot home in the center of the US may save approximately $300 in heating and $100 in air conditioning cost each year. In the northern parts of the US and in Canada, savings in heating will be lot more than cooling. In addition, the smaller equipment needed for such house can cut construction cost by an estimated $500 to $2,000.[8]

---

[8] http://www.forms.org/product_info/brief_energy.html

GREEN HOUSE: THE ENERGY EFFICIENT HOME

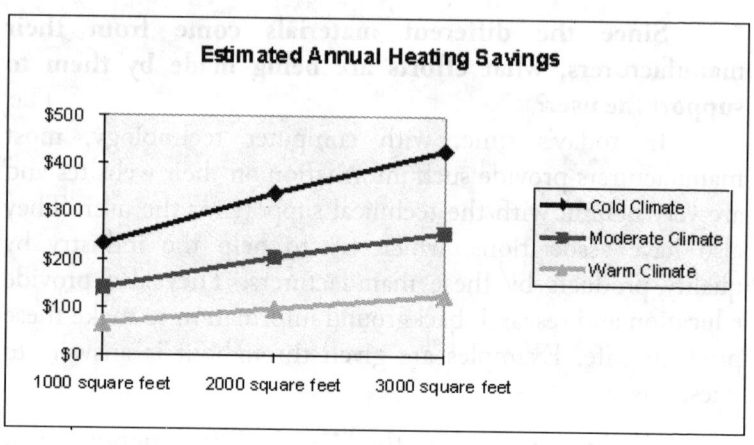

Where do these data come from?

The energy saving estimates come from a study of single-family houses spread across the US and Canada and is based on data on some 60 houses. Half had exterior walls constructed with concrete using ICFs made of expanded polystyrene (EPS) or extruded polystyrene (XPS) foam. The other half were neighboring houses with walls constructed of wood frame. All houses were relatively new (less than 6 years old) and built with modern methods. The energy bills of concrete house and its frame counterpart were compared and carefully corrected for important differences to get an "apples-to-apples" comparison. Estimates of equipment savings are actual numbers reported by contractors.

Where do the savings come from?

Insulation values for ICF walls using polystyrene foam range from R-17 to R-26, compared to wood frames from R-9 to R-15. ICF walls reduce the conduction losses through foundation and above-grade walls by about half. They are also built with denser concrete than the conventional fiberglass insulation, which allowed less than 50% less infiltration (air leakage) in the framed exterior walls.

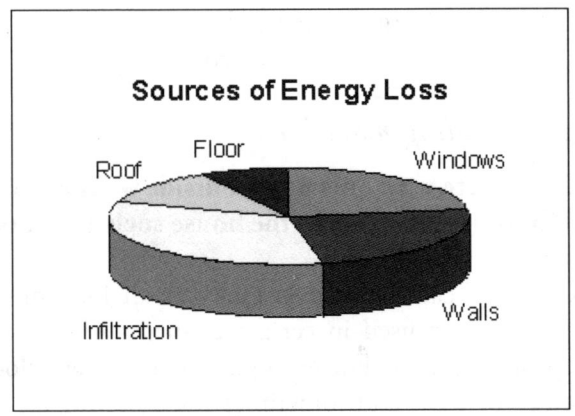

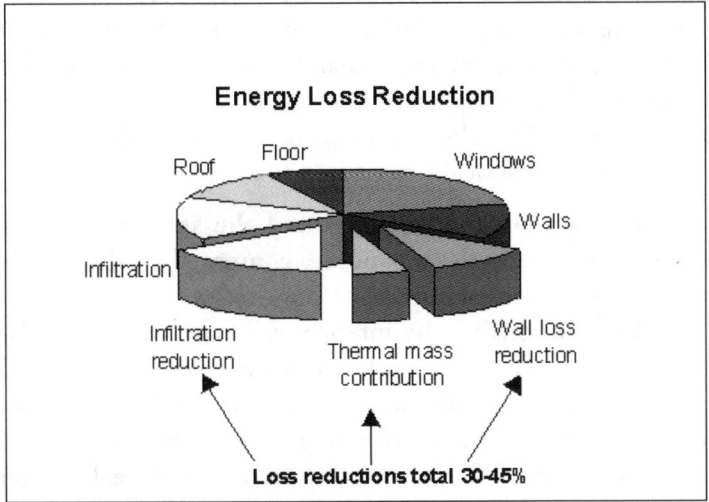

The concrete in ICF walls gives them the heat-absorbing property, or a "thermal mass". It keeps the walls of the house warmer when the outdoor temperature is at its coldest extreme and vice-versa. The walls themselves "add back" heating or cooling to the house when it needs them the most and this contributes about 6% of the needed energy to the house at no cost. Since the energy demand is less, the furnaces and compressors for heating and cooling are smaller.

Thus, more the energy savings, the greater is the possible reduction in equipment size and its cost.

Design *(including materials)*

Is concrete used only in the outside walls or can it also be used for other elements in the house such as floors or the staircase?

Concrete can be used virtually at all locations in the house. Concrete is used in certain elements of the house in one form or the other. For example, the basement floor slab, the footings of walls and sometimes the driveway are built in concrete. Concrete can be combined with recycled steel to gain more advantages. Making a composite floor system with recycled light gauge metal steel and concrete will substantially reduce the floor weight and also the noise from a squeaking wooden floor. Recycled steel can be used to build staircases much more economically compared to conventional ones.

In addition to the floors and the staircase, can the interior walls be built in concrete compared to the wooden walls in conventional homes?

Conventionally, the interior walls are built with 2"x4" frames with gypsum boards or sheet rock. These walls however suffer one main disadvantage in that they are hollow and transmit sound from one room to another. These walls can be replaced to save wood by using recycled steel sections; they are used typically in commercial construction. Alternately, lightweight concrete walls can be used (weighing as much as 75% less than conventional concrete); conduits for telephone and electrical wiring cables and piping may be incorporated within either alternate wall type. Lightweight concrete also provides a good sound barrier.

Are there any disadvantages of a concrete floor?

A concrete floor typically will be harder and somewhat colder compared to the conventional home. New technology is available to protect this concrete from being cold by using a thermal blanket. Until one gets used to a hard floor or a hardwood floor, one might find initially little discomfort; it can be minimized by using heavier padding if finishing in carpet. Use of carpet on concrete floors will make the floor substantially warmer than the cold tile floor. Hot water heating pipes can be incorporated into the concrete or hybrid floor construction.

Are steel studs safe from an electrical point of view compared to wooden studs?
Yes, they are. In fact it's easier to provide the outlets in steel or run the wiring in steel studs because they come with pre-made holes compared to wooden studs in which it's more difficult to drill the holes once the walls are finished.

Is concrete certified for its quality by any agency?
Yes. Compared to wood it is certified by the concrete manufacturer. Wood sections at the local hardware store are not typically guaranteed or warranted. Wooden sections may appear satisfactory but may be dry or under-cured and be susceptible to warping. Concrete on the other hand is produced in the plant and is delivered to the site and its quality is guaranteed by the manufacturer.

Why does concrete possess good quality?
Concrete is man-made with several ingredients, whose quality has been checked for individual quality. When it is made in the plant, its mix design is done by qualified individuals and pre-tested for quality. These individuals are professionals and recognized by national organizations such as 100 year old American Concrete Institute (ACI). Considerable research goes in to concrete production.

Is it a cement house or really a concrete house?
It is a concrete house since cement is only one ingredient of concrete. The main components of concrete are cement, sand, stone and water; often admixtures are added depending on the type of environment and to aid mixing. Air is added to protect concrete from freeze-thaw problems, and water reducers are added in order to make the concrete flow

better and to improve its quality. Portland cements are composed of calcium silicates. Cements set and harden by reacting chemically with water. During this reaction, called hydration, cement combines with water to form a stone like mass. When the paste (cement & water) is added to aggregates (sand & gravel or stone) the paste acts as an adhesive and binds the aggregates together to form concrete.

What are insulated concrete forms (ICF) and how are they used in multi-story buildings or townhouses?

ICF formwork provides insulation through specially designed Styrofoam blocks, made standard and are easy to assemble in the field. This technology has been used in multi-story homes, but not as much in townhouses where they're used with conventional block walls as a separation between two adjacent homes. Concrete walls and ICF between two homes indeed will make a better quality townhouse by providing a sound barrier.

Is a concrete home a problem in terms of its construction by the contractor for homeowner?

No, but problems may be expected, which are no different or more complicated than with a conventional home.

Concrete is much heavier than wood. Will that make my house heavier and will I need to do something about the floors, if the floors are made in concrete?

Concrete is certainly heavier than wood; however one can still benefit from its use. First, concrete can be used with recycled steel as a composite floor thereby reducing the weight required for load bearing substantially. Only about 2" of concrete will serve with recycled metal to provide a satisfactory floor design. Light weight concrete can be used to result in less weight. Using a composite structural floor will avoid unsightly columns in the basement and provide more usable open space.

Can energy efficiency be increased, by providing a better roof than the conventional?

Significant energy loss occurs through the roof. Attic air in a sloped-roof house gets heated and therefore on a warm day there is a constant mass of hot air which needs to be isolated from the air conditioned air in the rooms below the ceiling during the summer. The roof structure may be changed by eliminating the trusses and providing an insulated concrete roof which is a thick material using light weight concrete and air.

How much insulation do concrete walls provide?

Insulation provided by insulated concrete is generally given by an R Value. The Tables below gives various R values adapted from data given on a number of Internet sources including those given in the footnote. Two examples are given, one for a conventional wall and one for a concrete ICF wall.[9]

"R" Values for Materials of Construction

	Thickness	R-Value
Air Spaces		
Air space, bound normal materials 3-1/2" stud wall	¾"	0.91
Exterior air film	-	0.17
Interior air film	-	0.68
Masonry		
Concrete block	8"	1.11
Face brick	2½"	0.28
Cast in place concrete	8"	0.64
Stucco	1"	0.20
Common brick	2½"	0.5
Building Materials	-	
Asphalt shingles	-	0.44

---

[9] http://www.concretenetwork.com/concrete/homes/index.html?source=gooaw&kw=12a
http://www.admoyer.com/builderslibrary/lib.Rvaluesmain.html
http://coloradoenergy.org/procorner/stuff/r-values.html

GREEN HOUSE: THE ENERGY EFFICIENT HOME

	Thickness	R-Value
Bevel lap siding	½" x 8"	0.81
Fiber board sheathing	3/4"	2.10
Gypsum board	3/8"	0.32
Gypsum board	½"	0.45
Paneling / plywood base	¼"	0.31
Plywood	v	0.63
Plywood	5/8"	0.79
Insulation		
Cellulose (milled paper & wood pulp)	1"	3.4
Mineral fiber (rock, slag, glass)	3½"	11.00 - 13.32
Mineral fiber (rock, slag, glass)	6"	19.0 - 22.3
Perlite	1"	2.75
Polystyrene	3"	17.64
Ridged insulation board	¾"	2.10
Ridged insulation board	1"	5.88
Vermiculite	1"	2.13
Blue Dow Styrofoam	1"	5.0
Blue Dow Styrofoam	2"	10.0

Example of a Conventional Wall

Wall – Outside Air Film	0.17
Siding - Wood Bevel	0.80
Plywood Sheathing ½"	0.63
3½" Fiberglass Batt	11.00
½" Drywall	0.45
Inside Air Film	0.68
Total R-Value	**13.7**

Example Concrete Wall

Polystyrene – 2"	11.8
Wall - Outside Air Film	0.17
Cast in Place Concrete – 8"	0.64
Polystyrene – 2"	11.8
Inside Air Film	0.68
Total R-Value	**25.2**

What provision can be made to avoid cracks in concrete?

There are many reasons why concrete cracks. Many of these cracks do not affect structural integrity. The majority of concrete cracks usually occur due to improper design and construction practice. This includes omission of isolation & control joints, improper jointing practices, improper subgrade preparation, the use of very wet concrete or addition of water on the job, improper finishing and inadequate or curing. Concrete "shrinks" slightly as it hardens, therefore proper spacing of joints is most important.

Should one use a high performance, air-entrained concrete mix?

The concrete should be at least 4,000 psi, with 6% air-entrainment and lowest water-cement ratio with some admixtures. High-performance concrete is always good to use. High-performance concrete mixes can be designed for easy placement, so the contractor is not saddled with a hard-to-handle concrete mix.

Construction

Will there be any problem in putting the nails or hangers in the wall?

No. The walls are finished similarly to the conventional home. The main difference is that the metal studs replace the wooden studs in the interior walls to which the sheet rock is attached. In the insulated concrete exterior walls with a foam shell, metal or plastic "studs" are embedded similar to the conventional home at 16" on-center. This means that one can attach pictures or other appurtenances by locating the stud and attaching the picture in a similar fashion to the wooden stud.

Can one finish the concrete floor with hardwood?

Yes. Similar to a wooden floor, one may finish with granite, marble or another type of tile. The concrete floor provides a much more stable base than wood. The weight of the tiles typically requires additional support compared to the wooden floor. A smooth concrete floor will make finishing with tiles much easier.

Should the roof be in wood or can it also be made in concrete or another alternate material?

The roof can be made of an alternate material such as recycled steel or concrete panels; both are available at this time. Recycled steel trusses (compared to wooden trusses), are available, are lighter and cost less than wooden trusses. Construction of the roof may be different with steel trusses. Instead of placing a (wooden) truss one at a time, it is much easier to build an entire roof on the ground and then lifting it up in place by a crane. It is both efficient and economical. As far as a concrete roof is concerned, concrete panels can be made and supported and insulated, making the structure even more energy efficient. Insulation in the attic can be provided by recycled cotton fibers, which are available and provide a high insulation value. Compared to the conventional R-value of R-30, the recycled cotton insulation provides an R-value up to R-50 to improve efficiency further.

Are there any problems in constructing a concrete house compared to a wooden or a conventional house?

A: Not really. The main difference between the two types of construction will be due to the experience of the contractor. It's just a matter of time when the culture in residential construction will change to an improved, beautiful and long lasting home, which is made out of better construction material—concrete.

Can interior walls in a concrete house be built in a conventional fashion?

In concrete homes built with insulated concrete forms (ICF), walls may still be built of wood. Most inside non-load bearing walls can be built with lightweight concrete. Compared to a concrete with a density value of 150 lbs/ft^3, lightweight concrete weighs as little as 50 lbs/ft^3. Sound transmission will be considerably reduced compared to conventional walls.

Will alternate materials for wall construction pose any problem for the utilities such as telephone or electrical wiring?

Preplanning for utility locations and outlets is required for all types of construction, including alternate construction. Recycled steel sections for interior walls have holes placed at proper locations for electrical and telephone conduits. Non-load bearing conventional or alternate material walls may be moved equally easily. For exterior walls, conduits and outlets can be located within the foam formwork avoiding the concrete itself. Similarly, relocation may be done within the formwork.

Can staircases be made using the concept of steel/concrete working together?

Yes. In a house described in this book, recycled 2"x10" steel used for the floor beams and 2"x6" sections used for load bearing walls were used very effectively to build staircases on site during construction. Experience indicates that use of the sections resulted a saving of 60-70% compared to the cost of conventional staircases. The finishing was done conventionally using a wooden finish and carpeting with padding in the rest of the house. Most importantly, these staircases are sturdier than the conventional wood and like the concrete floors they do not either squeak or make noise during their use.

Can a concrete roof be pre-cast or pre-fabricated or must it be made at the site?
They come in both varieties, pre-made as well as poured in the field. Generally it is preferred to use the pre-made panels, which being lighter can be stacked, shipped and easily assembled.

What does "slump" mean?
Slump is an indication of how well the concrete flows. It indicates the quantity of water in the concrete mixture. The lower the slump, the less water is in the mix and the stronger the concrete will be. But low-slump concrete is harder to pour. The slump is measured by putting concrete in a 12" tall cone with a flat top, then pulling the cone up and allowing the concrete to slump down. The distance the concrete falls from the top of the cone to the top of the slumped concrete is the slump. With today's technology of admixtures, one can achieve higher slump with less water with the application of water reducers or super-plasticizers.

Why is reinforcement provided in concrete?
For concrete slabs, the primary purpose of reinforcement is to keep cracks closed tightly. The product normally used in this application is wire fabric, although success has been achieved using synthetic fibers.

What is fiber mesh and why are fibers used in concrete?
Fiber mesh is typically polypropylene (plastic) fibers introduced into the mix during the batching process. These fibers serve as a secondary reinforcement in the concrete. In most cases, fibers can replace welded wire fabric as a means of secondary reinforcement.

Can I replace wire mesh with fibers?

The answer depends on the intended purpose of installing wire mesh. If control joint spacing exceeds 30 times the concrete thickness, then wire mesh should be used to hold random cracks together. If control joint spacing does not exceed 30 times the concrete thickness, wire mesh can be omitted and fiber can be used to reduce surface cracking resulting from rapid evaporation (plastic shrinkage cracking) and improve fatigue strength.

What is a vapor retarder?

A vapor retarder is a material used to minimize the transmission of water from the soil through a concrete slab. A retarder is useful when the concrete will be covered with tile or floor coverings, and can help prevent radon penetration. Proper concrete placement is required to prevent problems with cracking, curling and delaminating due to confinement of bleed water.

When is it too cold to pour concrete?

Concrete will not set (or harden) when the concrete temperature is below about 35°F. Many times specifications will say something like *"Concrete may not be poured when the temperature is 37°F and falling."* With heated water and aggregates, accelerating admixtures, and other methods, jobs can be poured below freezing, but it is more costly. In most southern states in the US and in tropical latitudes there are so few or no freezing days that it is not worth it to try to pour when the temperature is below freezing.

Does one really need to put joints in the slab?

racks in concrete cannot be prevented, but can be controlled. Three basic types of joints include contraction, construction and isolation. Each has a specific purpose and use must be carefully planned. Depth and shape of the basement slab, columns or other artifacts in the construction are important factors to consider.

What are joints in concrete?

Joints are pre-planned cracks to accommodate the expansion and shrinkage of concrete from changes in moisture and temperature. Irregular cracks are unsightly and difficult to maintain, but do not generally affect the concrete integrity. Cracks in concrete can be controlled and minimized by properly designed joints.

How important is the sub-grade?

The sub-grade or the underlying support material is vital to the performance of a slab. The sub-grade should be graded to uniformly to result in uniform depth of concrete to avoid cracking. Soft areas should be removed to prevent unequal settlement. Proper drainage must be provided. The sub-grade must be free of frost before concrete is placed.

How important is curing?

Concrete should be cured for at least 7 days by keeping it continuously moist. This can be accomplished with fogging, ponding, application of curing compounds or covering with a barrier such as polyethylene sheeting. Cold and hot weather conditions require special procedures to prevent freezing and shrinkage cracking due to rapid evaporation respectively.

Other *(including aesthetics)*

How good is a concrete house from earthquake, wind or tornado protection?

A: A concrete house compared to the wooden one is just as safe in case of an earthquake. It will be even safer in the case of other hazards such as fire or wind. Fire alone causes property destruction of several billion dollars per year similar to that done by winds and tornados.

My floor seems to make a squeaking noise almost from the day we moved into the house, is concrete any better as an alternative material?

Squeaking in the house is often a problem with the wooden floor. As wood gets older, it can make noise because of the organic structure. Properly made and poured concrete will not squeak, and it will also make a better floor.

We hear the floor bouncing and making noise at the main level when someone is walking on the floor above. Can a concrete floor help this situation?

A concrete floor will not have such a problem because it is stiffer than the wooden floor. The additional advantage with a concrete floor is that it will provide a better sound barrier between the floors. Noise or music will not be easily transmitted to other floors or rooms.

Can a concrete home be finished either in conventional fashion or any special way? If it does, is there a big cost differential between the two?

Aesthetics of finishing homes is independent of the type of construction materials one uses during its construction. Many people buy the house because it looks attractive. Therefore, one might choose first the aesthetic and then put the construction to use for its best purpose.

If I'm building a driveway, should I look into a concrete driveway or should I consider an asphalt driveway?

There are indeed two choices. Concrete driveways are more beautiful compared to an asphalt driveway and less prone to maintenance, although they are a bit more expensive. It makes sense to match a concrete driveway with a concrete apron instead of two dissimilar materials of construction. The aprons near the roadway are built for a longer life compared to the driveway.

What benefits can one get by using concrete driveway instead of one with asphalt?
Consider the cost of the driveway over its lifetime. A good quality concrete driveway will last more than 30 years with little or no maintenance. Asphalt driveways need periodic sealing coats to retard-age related cracking. Even properly constructed residential asphalt driveways will deteriorate more quickly due to environmental influences than due to vehicle traffic. If one considers the cost of surface, crack sealers and the shorter life-span of the asphalt, concrete will prove to be very cost-effective. A properly placed concrete driveway has a much longer life expectancy than an asphalt driveway. A concrete driveway is much cooler in the summer months. Residue from an asphalt driveway can potentially be tracked into your home.

What is the minimum thickness of concrete driveway?
Often 2"x4"s are used to form driveways, which are only 3½ inches deep, so the ground inside the 2"x4" forming needs to be removed at least ½ inch below the bottom of the form. Thickness is the major factor in determining the driveway's structural capacity. Increasing it from 4" to 5" inches will add 20% to your concrete cost, while the additional inch of concrete will add almost 50% to load-carrying capacity of your driveway.

Energy Efficiency in Residential Construction

Introduction

A concrete home has an energy efficiency advantage and its use should increase in the residential markets. Also energy efficiency and the related economy bring another dimension of concrete.

Elements of an Energy-Efficient House

There is much to consider when designing and building an energy-efficient house. Recent developments and improvements in building elements and construction techniques allow most modern energy saving ideas to be seamlessly integrated into house designs. While the design costs, options, and styles vary, most energy efficient homes have some basic elements in common: a well constructed and tightly sealed thermal envelope; controlled ventilation; properly sized high- efficiency heating and cooling systems, and energy efficient doors, windows, and appliances.

A thermal envelope is everything about the house that serves to shield the living space from the outdoors. It includes the wall and roof assemblies, insulation, windows, and weather-stripping and caulking.

Some of the available and popular energy efficient construction methods include the following:

1. Value engineering methods use wood only where it is most effective, reducing cost and saving space for insulation. Although the amount of lumber has been determined to be structurally sound through experience and laboratory and field tests, the builder must be familiar with this type of construction to ensure a structurally sound house.

2. Structural insulated panels are sheets made of ply wood or oriented strand board that is laminated to form board. Since structural insulated panels act as both the framing and provide the insulation, construction is much faster than the typical value engineering or stick framing. The quality of construction is often superior because there are fewer opportunities for workers to make mistakes.
3. Houses with insulating concrete forms consist of two layers of extruded foam board (one inside and one outside of the wall) that act as the form for a steel reinforced concrete center. It's one of the fastest construction techniques and the least likely to result in construction mistakes. Such buildings are also very strong and easily exceed code requirements for areas prone to tornadoes or hurricanes.

An energy efficient house has much higher insulation R-values than required by most local building codes. An R-value is the ability of a material to resist heat transfer. The lower the value, the more rapid the heat loss! Carefully applied fiberglass batt or rolls, wet-spray cellulose, or foam insulation will fill wall cavities completely. Foundation walls and slabs should be as well insulated as the living space walls. Poorly insulated foundations have negative impact on home energy use and comfort. Also, appliances that supply heat as a byproduct are often located in the basement. By carefully insulating the foundation walls and the floor of the basement, the operation of these appliances can assist in heating the house.

Water vapor condensation is a major threat to the structure of a house, no matter what the climate. A vapor-retarder is a material or structural element that can be used to inhibit the movement of water vapor, while an air retarder can inhibit airflow into and out of a house's envelope. Regardless of climate, water vapor migration should be minimized by using a carefully designed thermal envelope and sound construction practices. Systems that control air and water vapor movement in homes rely on the nearly airtight installation of sheet materials on the interior as the main barrier. The airtight drywall approach may be used to satisfy these needs.

The typical home loses more than 25 percent of its heat through windows. Therefore, an energy-efficient house in a heating dominated climate should have few windows on all of its sides except for the south face. Use of windows and doors in a cooling dominated climate should be minimized. There are many manufacturers of windows and doors manufactured as inserts suitable for new construction and replacement of existing units that are highly resistant to heat flow through and around properly installed frameworks. The R-value and other energy efficiency data are always freely available from the manufacturers and vendors.

Air leaks should be sealed everywhere in a home's thermal envelope to reduce energy loss. Good air sealing alone may reduce costs by as much as 50 percent. Most air sealing can be accomplished by using caulking and weather-stripping. Since an energy-efficient house is tightly sealed, it may need to be ventilated in a controlled manner, in climates where windows are not often opened to the outside air. Controlled, mechanical ventilation helps reduce health risks from indoor air pollution, promotes a more comfortable atmosphere, and reduces air moisture infiltration.

Specifying the correct sizes for heating and cooling systems in airtight, energy efficient homes can be tricky. Rule of thumb sizing used for typical house construction is often inaccurate, resulting in cost-inefficient systems wasteful operation. Energy efficient homes require relatively small heating systems even in very cold climates. If an air conditioner is required, it's often a small unit and sufficient for most climates.

Appliances with relatively high operating efficiencies are usually more costly to purchase, however, higher efficiency appliances provide a measure of insurance against increases in energy prices, emit less air pollution, and are attractive selling points when the home is resold. Houses that incorporate energy efficient appliances are more comfortable and maintain a stable temperature, indoor humidity is better controlled, and drafts are reduced. They are also quiet because of extra insulation and tight construction.

The newest version of *EnergyPlus* (Version 1.2.2) was completed in April 2005 and is now available in versions for both Windows and Linux operating systems. *EnergyPlus* Version 1.2.2 can be downloaded at no cost from DOEs Energy Efficiency and Renewable Energy (EERE's) Building Technologies Program Web sites.[10] This website gives software, which will help in the planning process for those interested in pursuing mode detailed analysis on their own. More detailed information for home energy saving is available at[11] and especially for planning new homes at[12]:

In summary, an energy efficient home provides superior comfort and lower operating costs as well as a higher real estate market value.

Various Sources of Energy

There are many alternative energy sources and more on the horizon as energy consciousness continues to develop. Three of the popular ones for residential consideration are discussed herein, solar, earth embankment and geothermal.

Solar Energy[13]

Solar energy may be captured and utilized through the implementation of a photovoltaic system. Photovoltaic (PV) technology has been used to power homes in regions with significant sunlight for many years. Solar modules come in two distinct categories—crystalline silicon and amorphous

---

[10]http://www.eere.energy.gov/buildings/energyplus/
[11]http://www.eere.energy.gov/buildings/info/homes/index.html
[12]http://www.eere.energy.gov/buildings/info/homes/newconstruction.html
[13]http://www.eere.energy.gov/RE/solar_basics.html

silicon thin film. Both amorphous and crystalline technologies are commonly used in efficient grid-connected and stand-alone installations. Mono and poly crystalline modules usually have 36 solar cells in a 9x4 matrix connected in series to provide an output voltage suitable for battery charging. A typical module will provide a peak power output voltage of 17 volts and output current of 4.7 amps under optimum conditions. Modules can be connected in series or parallel to form an array to provide higher voltage and current outputs as required. Crystalline solar modules are covered with tempered glass on top and tough ethylene vinyl acetate (EVA) material at the back. The glass and backing material protect the solar cells from moisture. Crystalline modules need to stay cool. Efficiency of crystalline PV arrays decreases by 0.5 percent per degree Celsius above the "standard" operating temperature of 25°C. Good ventilation is required at the back of the modules. Exposure to cool breezes when placing the house is an important consideration.

Amorphous silicon is one of a number of thin film technologies used in photovoltaic systems. This type of solar cell can be applied as a film to support substrates such as glass or plastic. Advantages of thin film cells include easier disposal and assembly, low cost of substrates or building materials, as well as ease of production and suitability for larger applications. Although efficiency of thin film modules is lower than that of crystalline modules, both types of modules are cost competitive. Thin film modules have various coating and mounting systems. Some are less susceptible to damage from hail and other impacts than those covered in glass.

Solar modules can be supplied with a frame, usually constructed of anodized aluminum, or as an unframed laminate. More solar modules are being fabricated as building materials so that they can be integrated into the building's fabric. They include solar roof tiles, wall materials and semi-transparent roof material for atriums and skylights. It is anticipated that further development of thin film technology will lead to a proliferation of cost-effective PV coated building materials that can be integrated with the building's fabric to reduce costs. Solar modules produce most power when they are pointed directly at the sun. It is important to install them so that they receive maximum sunlight. Ideally, they should be in full sun from 9 a.m. to 3 p.m. in midwinter.

For stand-alone PV systems winter operation is crucial and therefore, the elevation angle should be the latitude plus 15°. For grid connected systems, the angle should be reduced from latitude by 10° to maximize the amount of energy produced annually. Essentially, if the main loads are in the winter months when solar exposure is reduced, tilt angles should be approximately equal to latitude plus 15° to maximize exposure to the low winter sun. If major loads are cooling and refrigerating, the tilt angle should be reduced to latitude minus 10°, the summer optimum angle.

Output power of an array of cells is directly proportional to power received from the sun. The rated maximum output of the module might only be achieved occasionally depending on the actual site. System designers calculate the output energy from the peak sun hours, which is a measure of the available solar energy. It is numerically equal to the daily solar radiation in kilowatt hours per square meter (kWh/m^2) and peak sun hours vary throughout the year. Output energy is usually averaged and presented as a monthly figure. The peak power output of modules is rated in kilowatt peak (kWp) and is measured under standard test conditions.

Shading one of the cells in a module is similar to opening a switch in a circuit and stopping the current from flowing. This results in a loss of power from many cells, not just the one that is shaded. Partial shading can cause "hot spots" that can damage the module. This occurs in mono and poly crystalline modules, but not in amorphous modules. Arrays should not be located near trees that will grow and shade the modules.

Standard solar modules are supplied with junction boxes on the back to facilitate electrical interconnection. Some modules used in grid connected systems now have leads and plugs/sockets for easier installation. Bypass diodes are supplied within junction boxes for mono and poly crystalline modules. These bypass diodes allow current to flow through them when cells are shaded, minimizing the possibility of damage from shading. Since at night the solar cells act as a resistance and current will flow from the battery pack into the module, blocking diodes should be installed in junction boxes to prevent this. In stand-alone PV's, the array needs to be installed as close as possible to the batteries to minimize the power loss between the modules and the batteries and the size of the cable will be determined by the system designer. If the array frame and the module frame are made of different metals they must be separated by an isolating material to prevent electrochemical corrosion.

True building integration requires that the PV product is either fully integrated into or replaces an existing building element. PV installations are currently a considerable additional expense, but if done well, building integrated PV modules should add considerable value to a home. Building integrated PV modules requiring few additional installation details beyond standard construction practice are beginning to appear. PV can be integrated into roofs, facades, skylights or awnings. Careful consideration in the design must be paid to the fact that many building integrated PV modules do not allow effective cooling of crystalline modules, resulting in lower output.

Earth–Sheltered Homes (Earth Embankment)[14]

The sheltered home is a very old idea indeed. It is instructive to review the concept and techniques for building an igloo if considering an earth sheltered home. A source for

---

[14]http://www.metaefficient.com/metaefficient/archives/building/earth-sheltered-houses.html

primary information is at: http://www.benmeadows.com/refinfo/Tips/Article1.html. An igloo can become very warm just from body heat. The structure is so "tight" from thawing and freezing of the outside surface that ventilation is essential. Some of the same considerations apply to earth sheltered homes.

Earth-sheltered construction can be an attractive and rewarding choice in housing. There are many advantages to earth-sheltered construction. An earth-sheltered home is less susceptible to the impact of extreme outdoor air temperatures, so one won't feel the effects of adverse weather as much as in a conventional house. Temperatures inside the house are more stable than in conventional homes, and with less temperature variability, interior rooms seem more comfortable. Earth-sheltered houses require less exterior maintenance, such as painting and cleaning gutters. Constructing a house dug into the earth or surrounded by earth provides some natural soundproofing. Finally, earth-sheltered houses may cost less to insure because their design offers extra protection against high winds, hailstorms, and natural disasters such as tornados and hurricanes.

There are a few disadvantages to earth-sheltered housing, including an initial cost of construction which may be 20 percent higher, the level of care required to avoid moisture problems, difficulties associated with reselling the house, and a few more hurdles in the mortgage application process. Earth sheltered designs may present some difficulty such as conformance to minimum window sizes in each room, roofing specifications, and insulation requirements specified by codes.

There are two basic types of earth sheltered housing - underground or embanked with the imported or outside earth. Underground housing means an entire structure is built below grade or completely underground. Such a structure may be above grade or partially below grade, with outside earth surrounding one or more walls. Both types usually have earth covered roofs, and may have a vegetation cover to reduce erosion. From these two basic types, three general designs have been developed. They are:

1. **Atrium style** - an underground structure where an atrium serves as the focus of the house and the entry to the home.
2. **Elevation style** - a structure that may have a south-facing entry with glass.
3. **Partially embanked style** - a structure which is built above grade and is sloped to shelter the exterior walls not facing south.

The atrium design is built completely below ground on a flat site and the major living spaces surround a central outdoor courtyard. The windows and glass doors that are on the exposed walls facing the atrium provide light, solar heat, outside views, and access via a stairway from the ground level. Atrium/courtyard homes are usually covered with less than 3 ft of earth primarily because there is no benefit in energy efficiency from greater depths. This design is ideal for an area without scenic exterior views, in dense developments, and on sites located in noisy areas. However, passive solar gain might be more limited, and courtyard drainage and snow removal are important items to consider in design.

The first two types are more conventional earth sheltered housing designs.

Elevation style plans expose one whole face of the house and cover the other sides and perhaps the roof with earth. The covered sides protect and insulate the house. The exposed front of the house, usually facing south, allows the sun to light and heat the interior. The floor plan is arranged so common areas and bedrooms share light and heat from the southern exposure. This type of house is usually set into the side of a hill at varying depths and can be the least expensive and simplest to build of all earth sheltered structures. This design may have limited internal air circulation and reduced daylight in the northern portions of the house, although there are ways to alleviate these problems by using skylights.

In the penetration style, the earth covers the entire house, except where it is retained for windows and doors. The house is usually built at ground level, and earth is embanked around and on top of it. This design allows cross-ventilation opportunities and access to natural light from more than one side of the house.

The climate in region will determine whether an earth-sheltered house can be a practical housing solution. Studies show that they are more cost-effective in climates that have significant temperature extremes and low humidity. The site topography and microclimate determine how easily the house can be surrounded with earth. A modest slope requires more excavation than a steep one, and a flat site is the most demanding, because it needs extensive excavation. A south-facing slope in a region with moderate to long winters is ideal for an earth sheltered building. In regions with mild winters and predominantly hot summers, a north-facing slope might be ideal. Although there is some variation, generally southern exposures offer more sun and daylight throughout the year than north-facing. Some types of soil are more suitable than others for earth-sheltered construction. As an example, the best soils are granular, sand and gravel. These soils compact well for bearing the weight of the construction materials and are very permeable, allowing for quick drainage. The poorest soils are cohesive, like clay, which may expand when wet and have poor permeability. Radon levels are another factor to consider in locating your home. Although, areas with high concentrations of radon can be hazardous, there are methods that can reduce radon buildup in both conventional and earth-sheltered dwellings.

The groundwater level at the site is another important consideration. Building above the water table is essential. Choosing a site where the water will naturally drain away from the building is the best way to avoid water pressure against the underground walls. The site should be surveyed for low spots and areas where water will collect. Seasonal or regular surface water flows should be channeled away from the structure. Drainage systems must be designed to draw water away from the structure and underground footing drains similar to those required by a house with a basement are necessary in many cases.

Waterproofing can be a challenge in earth-sheltered construction. Several waterproofing systems are currently in use, including rubberized asphalt, plastic and vulcanized sheets, liquid polyurethanes, and bentonite.

1. Rubberized asphalt combines a small amount of synthetic rubber with asphalt and is coated with a polyethylene layer to form sheets. It can be applied directly to walls and roofs and has a long life expectancy.
2. Plastic and vulcanized sheets are among the most common types of underground waterproofing. Plastic sheets include high-density polyethylene, chlorinated polyethylene, polyvinyl chloride, and chloro-sulfonated polyethylene.
3. Liquid polyurethanes are often used in places where it is awkward to apply a membrane.
4. Bentonite is natural clay formed into panels or applied as a liquid spray. The panels are simply nailed to walls and then the spray is mixed with a binding agent and applied to underground walls. When bentonite comes in contact with moisture it expands and seals out the moisture.

Construction materials for each type of structure will vary, depending on characteristics of the site, climate, soils, and design. Concrete is the most common choice for constructing earth-sheltered buildings. Not only is it strong, it is also durable and fire resistant. Lightly reinforced concrete which is poured and reinforced at the site is used for non-critical structural elements such as concrete foundations, floor slabs, and exterior walls with less than 6 ft of earth cover. Pre-cast reinforced concrete can resist loads at any reasonable depth and can be used for floors, walls, and roofs. Concrete absorbs and stores heat, helping to prevent temperature swings that can damage some building materials. Pre-cast concrete components are cured at a plant or on site before they are used, thereby decreasing construction time and cost in comparison to cast-in-place forms. The uses and advantages of pre-cast and cast-in-place concrete are similar, except that pre-cast concrete works best in simple or repeatable shapes. Special care must be taken to make the joints between sections watertight. Masonry, wood, and steel may also be used in earth-sheltered construction.

Humidity levels may increase in earth-sheltered houses during the summer, which can cause condensation on the interior walls. Installing insulation on the outside will prevent the walls from cooling down to earth temperature; however, it also decreases the walls' summer cooling effect. Mechanical air conditioning or a dehumidifier is often necessary to solve the humidity issue. Although insulation in an underground building does not need to be as thick as that in a conventional house, it is necessary to make an earthen house comfortable. Insulation is usually placed on the exterior of the house after applying the waterproofing material, so the heat generated, collected, and absorbed by the earth-sheltered envelope is retained inside the building's interior. If insulating outside the wall, a protective layer of board should be added to keep the insulation from contacting the earth. Adequate air exchange must be carefully planned when building an earth-sheltered dwelling. Well planned, natural ventilation or ventilation by exhaust fans can dissipate ordinary odors. Any combustion appliances that are installed should be "sealed combustion units," which have their own, direct source of outside air for combustion, and the combustion gases are directly vented to the outside.

Earth sheltered homes provide many energy efficient features that will provide a comfortable, tranquil, weather-resistant atmosphere. They can protect from the elements and the rising costs of energy and building resources.

Geothermal Energy[15]

For the homeowner or building owner anywhere in the United States, the emergence of geothermal heat pumps brings the benefits of geothermal energy to everyone's doorstep. The concept underlying all the ways geothermal energy is very simple and is used to benefit from the thermal energy available from beneath the surface of the earth.

There are several types of geothermal resources including hydrothermal, geo-pressured, hot dry rock, magma and earth energy.

1. Hydrothermal resources are reservoirs of steam or hot water, which are formed by water seeping into the earth and collecting in and being heated by fractured or porous hot rock.
2. Geo-pressured resources are deeply buried waters at moderate temperature that contain dissolved methane. While technologies are available to tap geo-pressured resources, they are currently not economically competitive.
3. Hot dry rock resources occur at depths of five to 10 miles everywhere beneath the earth's surface and at shallower depths in certain areas. Access to these resources involves injecting cold water down one well, circulating it through hot fractured rock, and drawing off the now hot water from another well. No commercial applications are in use at this time.
4. Magma offers extremely high temperature geothermal opportunities, but existing technology does not allow use of heat from this resource.

---

[15] http://www.eere.energy.gov/RE/geo_basics.html

5. Earth energy is the heat contained in soil and rocks at shallow depths from 3 to 200 feet. This resource is generally used as conventional geothermal energy with heat pumps and is the most common choice for residential application at this time.

Technologies have evolved that allow utilization of this heat. Homeowners can use the earth as a heat source or heat sink with geothermal heat pumps. According to the U.S. EPA, geothermal heat pumps are one of the nation's most efficient heating, cooling, and water-heating systems available. Homeowners who have installed geothermal heat pumps are not only doing their part to help make the world a cleaner place, they are also being rewarded with low operating and maintenance costs as well as low life cycle costs. The heat pump investment may cost more than $20 per month more in mortgage payments, but it may save $40 per month on their electric bill (2005). Although the geothermal heat pump does not create electricity, it greatly reduces consumption of it. The system uses electricity to move thermal energy between the building and the ground and reduces consumption of electricity by 30 to 60 percent compared to traditional heating and cooling systems. This reduction allows a payback of system installation in less than 10 years. The systems have life cycles of 30+ years.

Additional Alternatives in Energy Efficient Construction

There are many ways to increase the energy efficiency of a residential structure. Some additional techniques include, but are not limited to, the following:

1. **Landscaping for Energy Efficiency** is a cost-effective, yet eye-pleasing way to lower energy costs. Planting trees, shrubs, vines, grasses, and hedges are viable options. Landscaping may be the best long term investment for reducing heating and cooling

costs, while bringing other improvements to the community. A well designed landscape will:
- Cut your summer and winter energy costs dramatically.
- Protect your home from winter wind and summer sun.
- Reduce consumption of water, pesticides, and fuel for landscaping and lawn maintenance.
- Help control noise and air pollution.

2. Wind Systems can help owners take advantage of a growing amount of renewable electricity being harnessed from the wind.
3. Micro Hydro units convert the energy of flowing water into electrical energy. The energy produced by them is renewable, and the process does not emit polluting gases. In micro hydro systems, water turns a wheel or runner (like a propeller) to rotate a turbine and produce electricity. Micro hydro power is best where water supply is continuously available.
4. Efficient batteries and inverters are required to turn renewable energy sources into electricity. A complete renewable energy system has a number of components including a grid connect inverter, switchboard, and electricity meter. Owners and builders should do considerable research on each component before making a selection for their system.

Government vs. Private Role in Energy-Efficient Construction

Over 100 million homes in the United States account for approximately 20 percent of the nation's carbon dioxide emission (EPA 2000)[16]. Addition of about 1.4 million per year new homes are indicates that there is a staggering responsibility for both government and private stakeholders to increase energy efficiency in home construction. Efforts to improve home energy efficiency will go a long way toward reducing greenhouse gas emissions and other energy-related pollution.

Federal, state, and local agencies have an increasing responsibility to gather technical information to prepare inventories of greenhouse gas emissions (and other related pollution), develop action plans to reduce emissions and educate their constituents. They should emphasize the economic and environmental benefits of energy efficiency and encourage their constituents to implement voluntary measures to reduce their greenhouse gas emissions.

Although energy costs are the second-highest expense for homeowners after mortgage payments, many homebuyers may not even consider energy consumption when comparing prospective houses (EPA 2000). Many homeowners and contractors may be reluctant to invest in energy improvements due to lack of information and/or understanding, or may not believe they can finance upgrades. In such cases, states can help remove such barriers by encouraging the use of home energy rating systems and working with lenders on loan products that promote energy efficiency. ENERGY STAR[17]

---

[16] The estimate should include exhaled carbon dioxide as well as energy management sources.

[17] ENERGY STAR is a dynamic voluntary government and industry partnership that makes it easy for businesses and consumers to save money and protect the environment. In 1991, the US Environmental Protection Agency introduced the Green Lghts program, a voluntary program that encouraged organizations to upgrade their lighting to energy efficiency lighting systems and controls. The labeling program was launched the following year and the ENERGY STAR brand was introduced. The ENERGY STAR brand identifies energy-efficient products and promotes energy performance that saves energy and protects the environment. In 1996, EPA partnered with Department of Energy to increase the product offerings of the ENERGY STAR label. The label was expanded to include new homes, commercial and institutional buildings, residential heating and cooling equipment, major appliances, office equipment, lighting, and

products may also be used in conjunction with rating systems and loan products. An energy-efficient mortgage is also a viable financial product for the advancement of energy efficiency in the home. Such investments in home energy efficiency, for homeowners and contractors alike, prove valuable. An EPA-funded study determined that energy-efficient homes have a higher market or resale value regardless of how long the home is owned. Home value increases $20 for every $1 reduction in average annual utility bill. A typical ENERGY STAR home reduces utility bills by $420 per year; such savings can possibly add $8,400 to the market value of the home! (EPA 2000)

The federal government has taken steps to fulfill its responsibilities in promoting energy efficiency in the home. The U.S. Department of Energy supports state efforts to create home energy rating systems, and the U.S. EPA provides support through the Residential Energy Services Network (RESN) and the National Home Energy Rating Systems Council (NHERSC). The council has developed national home energy rating guidelines. The Federal Housing Administration has offered energy-efficient mortgages nationwide since October 1995. Fannie Mae, Freddie Mac, and the Veteran's Administration also offer energy efficiency loan products. In addition, the EPA/DOE ENERGY STAR Homes Program created special loan products for homes that meet the five-star rating. A growing number of leading mortgage lenders offer ENERGY STAR mortgages which feature a combination of incentives such as discounted interest rates and closing costs. (EPA 2000)

---

consumer electronics. Green Lghts, ClimateWise, and all labeled products have been consolidated under one umbrella; ENERGY STAR.

Economics in Concrete/Energy-Efficient Homes

Economics in Residential Homes

Economics is the use of scarce resources available to maximize the unlimited wants of human beings, which in turn brings satisfaction. There are three basic sectors in economics and these are household, business and government. These sectors are directly related in a circular flow such that the business sector (which embodies the resource and product markets) receives land, labor, capital and entrepreneurial ability from the household sector for its daily operation. The household sector in return receives income as well as goods and services. Income from the household is transferred to the business sector though the purchase of good and services. The government sector, which consists of the federal, state and local, forms the bridge between the business and household sectors and also supports them by providing goods and services whilst receiving net taxes in return.

Though the three sectors are interrelated, each can greatly affect the operation of the others either positively or negatively. Demand from the household is the key component responsible for changes in the other two sectors. Economic demand on households is affected by the price of the commodity, income, expected future demands, consumer taste, and the class of the household.

The household consists of a person(s) living in a residential facility with the responsibility of meeting (all) the domestic challenges. An average residential home receives some amount of satisfaction through the consumption of goods and services such as lighting, heating and cooling, water heating and the use of appliances provided by the business sector.

In the quest of gaining satisfaction many residential homes fall victim to wasting energy, hence raising their consumption levels as opposed to their income. Some of the ways through which energy is wasted in a home are:

1. Leakage through building envelop (window, walls, ceiling, doors etc)
2. Size of spacing requiring heating and cooling;
3. Amount of water heating needed and supplied;
4. Amount of wastewater produced;
5. Number of appliances and frequency of use;
6. Amount of garbage disposed; and
7. Lighting.

To cut back on energy consumption or wastage, an existing residential home must be improved to make it energy efficient. The focus must chiefly be on ensuring proper installation of all home fittings with good insulation, notwithstanding using energy efficient equipments or appliances at the time of renovation. The second concern is to regulate the use of energy in terms of lighting, heating and cooling, water heating, wastewater, etc.

For a new home construction, homeowners can take advantage of a concept known as "Whole Building Design (WBD)". This concept takes an integrative approach to building design so that all elements of the building help achieve an optimal energy performance. The building has to interact effectively with the outdoor environment — a concept known as climate-responsive architecture. "Whole Building Design" combines energy efficiency with solar technologies to boost energy savings and it reduces the amount of energy required to operate a home compared to conventional houses. The energy efficiency aspect of WBD is concerned with the same areas as mentioned with existing homes. The solar technologies incorporated into the WBD involves the use of Passive Solar Design and Solar Thermal Technology:

1. **Passive Solar Design** is the technology of heating, cooling, and lighting a building naturally with sunlight rather than with mechanical systems. Some design features include large south-facing windows and building materials that absorb and slowly release

the sun's heat. It can also involve the use of Photovoltaic (PV) technology. PV is basically "solar electricity" that results from converting sunlight into energy. PV systems help preserve the Earth's finite fossil-fuel resources such as coal, oil, and natural gas. It also helps reduce air and water pollution associated with these energy sources. Incorporating passive solar designs can reduce heating bills as much as 50 percent.

2. **Solar Thermal Technology** is the use of solar water-heating systems. These systems use collectors generally mounted on a south-facing roof. These collectors heat water either passively or actively (active being the most energy efficient).[2]

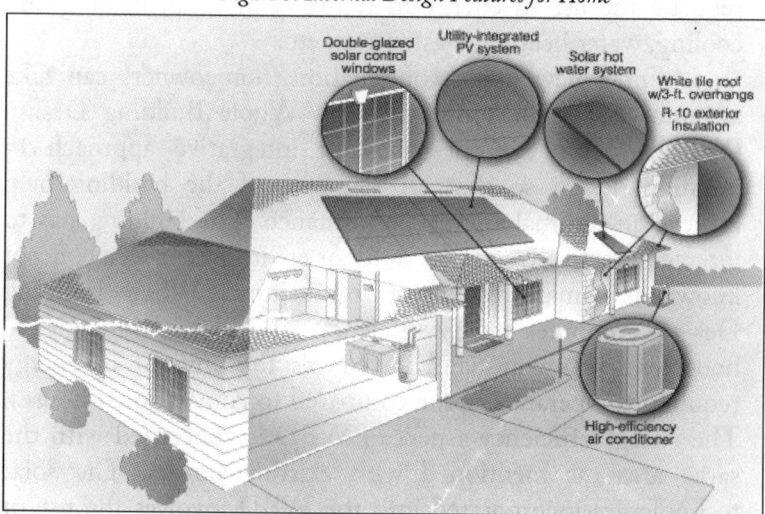

Figure 3. Internal Design Features for Home

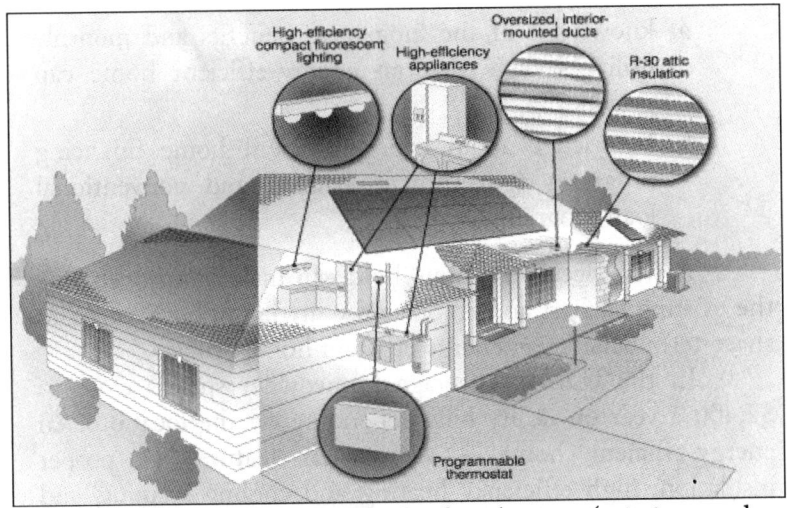

Across the U.S., relatively few homes (existing and under new construction) are energy efficient. Considering the environmental benefits that an energy-efficient home creates, it is curious that more people have not chosen to make their homes energy efficient.

The answer is in twofold:

1. The Human Barrier: reluctance on the part of consumers to undertake the conversion of their homes to energy efficient
2. Money: the upfront costs that are required to make the conversion are often too great a barrier for the average consumer to overcome. Also some energy efficiency improvements involve little or no implementation cost. Replacing a heating system can cost up to $5,000 in a large house or even more if you are converting from electricity to another energy source. Installing new windows, while very beneficial to your home and the environment can be a financial strain to implement.

The remedy to the above barriers is simply through:

a. knowledge of the long-term benefits and monthly utility savings that an energy-efficient home can provide.
b. knowledge about energy-efficient home financing programs (government backed and conventional loan programs).

A wise decision a household can make is to overcome the existing barriers and embrace the myriad of both long and short-term benefits an energy efficient home brings.

In the U.S. the average homeowner spends close to $2,400 a year on utility bills depending on the location. An energy-efficient home - with such features as proper insulation, high-efficiency heating and cooling systems, and energy-efficient windows - can lower utility bills 10 to 50 percent.

Government Legislation and Tax Incentives

There is some progress made at the federal government level. In August 2003 the House of Representatives passed the Omnibus Federal Energy Bill[3], but still has not been acted by the Senate. One needs to work on this by pushing his/her senator for action. This bill contains several tax credit provisions aimed squarely at residential real estate. It provides federal tax credits for homeowners who install energy conservation items such as:

- New insulation
- Energy-efficient windows
- Doors
- Solar hot water
- Photovoltaic equipment

For owners of existing homes the credit will be as much as 20 percent of the amounts spent on "Qualified Energy Efficiency Improvements," up to a maximum credit of $2,000. Tax credits are more valuable to taxpayers than deductions because they are subtracted dollar-for-dollar off the bottom line of a taxpayer's federal tax bill. There is separate credit available for the installation of solar and photovoltaic energy-production equipment. These tax credits are similar to the credits for conservation with a maximum allowable credit of $2,000 during a tax year. Under this bill, home builders and contractors also get a shot at tax relief. When they install energy-efficient heating and cooling systems in a new home they are constructing, they may be able to qualify for up to a $2,000 credit per home. These new federal tax credits could be very useful in promoting energy-efficient homes. The congressional Joint Committee on Taxation estimates that the home improvement incentives alone will lead to $1.6 billion worth of tax credits to homeowners in the coming decade. The solar and photovoltaic credits are estimated to put $125 million back into homeowners' pockets during the same period.

Federal involvement in the effort to encourage energy-efficient homes would mainly be in the form of tax incentives. Tax-based incentives are a flexible tool to help innovative energy-efficient technologies become competitive in the market. Tax-incentives help diminish market barriers by making new technologies more affordable, and thus lowering the risk of production (and the cost of financing) for manufacturers. As production and sales increase, the technologies will become available and affordable and tax credits can be phased out. Incentives to make building "envelopes" and air conditioners more efficient will reduce peak electricity demand, thus lowering electricity prices.

Support from various tax-based incentives for the innovative energy-efficient technologies listed below can enhance the use of such homes:

1. **New Homes** - A tax credit for highly efficient new homes will encourage builders to adopt energy-efficient building practices. In the long term, it will lower housing costs and save energy.

2 **Existing Homes** - A capped tax credit to assist with the cost of achieving energy-efficient upgrades will lower housing costs for American families and increase efficiency in the more than 100 million existing homes.

3 **Efficient Appliances** - A tax credit for manufacturers of highly efficient washing machines and refrigerators will help save energy and water. Environmentalists, efficiency advocates, and manufacturers support such a credit.

Tax incentives can be in the form of tax credits, which are directly subtracted from income tax that is owed; tax deductions, which reduce taxable income; or favorable treatment under various tax rules, such as an accelerated depreciation rate. Federal tax incentives have some operational advantages over federal programs - they are enacted for multi-year periods rather than being subject to annual appropriations and they do not require a separate bureaucracy as they are implemented by the Internal Revenue Service.

Government Programs for Energy-Efficient Homes

The government, as the bridge connecting the business and household sectors, has developed programs to increase consumer interest in energy-efficient homes. The only way to "encourage" widespread use of this type of housing is through Governmental Legislation requiring energy-efficiency and tax incentives.

Home Energy Rating Program

A home energy rating program outlines the criteria by which a home qualifies for energy-efficient financing. A professional energy rater who is certified under a nationally or state accredited Home Energy Rating System (HERS)[4] inspects the rating. An energy rater will inspect certain energy-related features of a home such as:

- insulation levels
- window efficiency
- heating and cooling systems
- air leakage

After inspection, the inspector will generate a report that includes the home's energy rating along with an estimation of annual energy use and costs. To help qualify for most energy-efficient financing, the report usually must show that the home is energy-efficient any recommended improvements are cost-effective and will save more money than what would needed to be borrowed. While calculating whether a borrower qualifies for a mortgage, a lender can recognize these savings and add the cost of the improvements into the mortgage or if the home is already energy-efficient, the lender can stretch the debt-to-income qualifying ratio (a borrower's monthly payment obligation on long-term debts divided by the borrower's net effective income or gross monthly income). An energy rater will inspect the energy-related features of a home, such as insulation levels, window efficiency, heating and cooling systems, and air leakage.

Financing Programs for Energy-efficient Homes

Energy-efficient financing[18] is offered through either government-insured or conventional loan programs. With these financing programs, there are two types of energy-efficient mortgages:

1. For a New Home
2. For an Existing Home

Government Insured

1 U.S. Department of Housing and Urban Development
- FHA Energy-Efficient Mortgage

---

[18] http://www.forms.org/info_sources/EEM/EEM.html

- FHA Section 203(k) Rehabilitation Mortgage Insurance
- FHA Energy-Efficient Home Mortgage
- FHA Mortgage Increase for Solar Thermal Systems
- FHA Title I Property Improvement Loan Insurance

2 U.S. Department of Veterans Affairs
- The U.S. Department of Veterans Affairs (VA) guarantees mortgage loans for veterans.
- It can be used to purchase or refinance a home along with the cost of making energy-efficient improvements.

3. U.S. Department of Housing and Urban Development

Under the U.S. Department of Housing and Urban Development (HUD), the Federal Housing Authority (FHA) insures mortgage and home improvement loans, for borrowers who would not otherwise qualify for conventional loans on affordable terms, such as some first-time home buyers and some residents of disadvantaged neighborhoods.

4. FHA Energy-Efficient Mortgage

FHA allows borrowers to finance the cost of adding energy-efficient improvements to new or existing homes as part of their FHA-insured purchase or refinancing mortgage.
- Energy-efficient improvement costs of $4,000 or 5 percent of the property value (up to $8,000), whichever is greater, can be financed.
- The FHA maximum mortgage limit for an area may be exceeded by the cost of the improvements.

- No additional down payment is required.
- No re-qualifying is necessary.
- No new appraisal is needed.
- Up to $200 of the cost of a home energy rating may be included in the mortgage.

This EEM can be used in conjunction with several other FHA-insured mortgages, including the 203(k) rehabilitation mortgage insurance described below.

5. FHA Section 203(k) Rehabilitation Mortgage Insurance

The FHA Section 203(k) rehabilitation mortgage insurance provides a borrower with a single loan that covers both the purchase or refinancing and the cost of major home improvements, including those that save energy. The program allows borrowers to complete improvements after the loan closes. The funds are placed in an escrow account and released as improvements are made.

- Total cost of improvements must exceed $5,000.
- The total property value must still fall within the FHA mortgage limit for the area. (The property value is determined by whichever is less: the value before the rehabilitation plus the cost of the rehabilitation or 110 percent of the appraised value after rehabilitation.)

6. FHA Energy-Efficient Home Mortgage

When purchasing an energy-efficient home, an FHA-approved lender can stretch the borrower's debt-to-income ratio by 2 percent.

7. FHA Mortgage Increase for Solar Thermal Systems

The maximum loan limit under FHA's standard 203(b) or 203(k) property rehabilitation mortgage insurance can be more than 20 percent if the home has or will have a passive or active solar heating system. The home must also have a 100 percent operational, conventional backup system.

8. **FHA Title I Property Improvement Loan Insurance**

   FHA also insures home improvement loans, including those that will make a home more energy efficient for homeowners with FHA-insured mortgages. It features:
   - Loans up to $25,000 for a single-family home
   - Loans insured up to 20 years
   - No required home energy rating reports.

9. **U.S. Department of Veterans Affairs**

   The U.S. Department of Veterans Affairs (DVA) guarantees mortgage loans for veterans with active duty service and qualified reservists. Its EEM can be used to purchase or refinance a home along with the cost of making energy-efficient improvements. To cover the cost of the improvements, the loan amount can be increased:
   - Up to $3,000 based solely on documented costs
   - Up to $6,000 if the increase in the mortgage payment is offset by the expected reduction in utility costs
   - More than $6,000 based on a value determination by VA

   A VA refinancing loan may not exceed 90 percent of the home's appraised value plus the costs of the improvements.

Private Sector Incentives

Conventional Programs

Most of the national lenders who offer energy-efficient financing operate through one of the following programs.

- ENERGY STAR® Mortgage
- Fannie Mae
- Freddie Mac
- E Seal

Energy STAR® Mortgage[19]

The Energy STAR® Homes program - sponsored jointly by the U.S. Department of Energy (DOE) and the Environmental Protection Agency (EPA) promotes voluntary partnerships with home builders to construct new homes that are 30 percent more efficient than the guidelines established by the Model Energy Code, which is a "model" national standard for residential energy efficiency.

The program also encourages lenders to provide EEM's for certified ENERGY STAR® homes. An ENERGY STAR® mortgage offers a minimum 2 percent stretch on a borrower's debt-to-income ratio plus at least one additional incentive for borrowers. Incentives may include:

- A lower interest rate
- A discount on closing costs and/or origination fees
- Up to a 4 percent extension of the debt-to-income ratio stretch
- Paying for the cost of the home energy rating

Fannie Mae

Fannie Mae, a private, shareholder-owned corporation operates under a congressional charter that directs it to channel efforts into increasing the availability and affordability of homeownership. It does not lend money directly to home buyers it purchases mortgages from lenders, ensuring that funds are available.

Energy-Efficient Mortgage

Fannie Mae encourages lenders to offer its EEM by providing incentives and specific criteria for those that it is

---

[19]http://www.energystar.gov/index.cfm?c=bldrs_lenders_raters.pt_HowConvey CostAdv

willing to purchase from lenders. Both existing and new homes fall under this EEM.

- Several approved home energy rating methods and programs, not just HERS, are allowed to evaluate a home's energy-efficiency.
- For existing homes, the cost of improvements is limited to 15 percent of its total cost. There is no limit imposed on the cost of improvements for new construction.
- A home buyer can finance 100 percent of the energy efficiency improvements without increasing the down payment.

Residential Energy Efficiency Improvement Loan

Fannie Mae is partnering with utility companies to provide loans to utility customers for the installation of energy-efficient home improvements. The loans feature:

- A below-market interest rate
- An unsecured financing option
- Up to $15,000
- A term of up to 10 years
- A "whole house" or bundled approach to efficiency improvements

Freddie Mac

Freddie Mac is a stockholder-owned, congressionally chartered corporation that works to create a continuous flow of funds to mortgage lenders in support of homeownership and rental housing. It purchases mortgages from lenders and packages them into securities that are sold to investors, providing homeowners and renters with lower housing costs and better access to home financing.

Energy-Efficient Mortgage (EEM)

Like Fannie Mae, Freddie Mac provides incentives, criteria, and flexible guidelines, for EEM's that encourage lenders to offer them to homeowners However, the EEM's are limited to purchasing existing energy-efficient homes or those to be either retrofitted or renovated.

- Several home energy rating methods and/or documentation, not just a HERS report are acceptable.
- Lenders can exceed the standard 2 percent debt-to-income stretch at their own discretion.
- It allows a broader range of energy-efficient improvements than most EEM programs.

E-Seal

E-Seal, an Edison Electric Institute program provides energy-efficient solutions for home buyers, residential energy customers, small business customers, and home builders.

Energy Efficiency Mortgage

This EEM is available through utilities with E Seal certified programs. It can be used to finance the purchase of a new home with energy-efficiency upgrades or to refinance an existing home while adding these improvements. It features:

- 100% financing of energy-efficiency upgrades
- No additional down payment, mortgage insurance obligation or re-qualification
- Maximum qualifying ratios that are 5% better than standard ratios and 3% better than regular EEM's
- Lower than prevailing market interest rates and closing costs.

Residential Financing Program

For energy-efficient home improvement loans, E-Seal's program participates with Fannie Mae's Residential Energy Efficiency Improvement Loan program (see above). When it comes to competent energy-efficient financing (mortgage) (EEM) whether you want to purchase, refinance or remodel a home it is best to work with lenders and/or real estate agents who are familiar with home energy ratings and program requirements. If you would like a home energy rating report, it is also best to work with a certified energy rater. In all instances, you should ask for references and check companies with your local better business bureau.[20]

Table 1 How An EEM Saves Money

	Standard Mortgage	New EEM
Energy Improvement Costs	-	$3,000
Appraisal Value	$100,000 (add cost of improvement)	$103,000
Down Payment	$10,000	$10,000
Mortgage Amount	$90,000	$93,000
P & I	$614	$634
Energy Savings (Monthly)	$0	$(50)
Total Monthly Payments	$614	$584

---

[20] http://www.pueblo.gsa.gov/cic_text/housing/energy_mort/energy-mortgage.htm

Table 2 How EEM Increases Buying Power

For A Standard Home Without Energy Improvements

Buyer's total monthly income	$3,000	$5,000
Maximum allowable monthly payment 28 percent debt-to-income ratio:	$840	$1,400
Maximum mortgage at 90 percent of appraised home value:	$132,900	$221,500

For An Energy-efficient Home

Buyer's total monthly income	$3,000	$5,000
Maximum allowable monthly payment 30 percent debt-to-income ratio:	$900	$1,500
Maximum mortgage at 90 percent of appraised home value:	$142,400	$237,300
Added Borrowing Power Due to the Energy-Efficient Mortgage:	$9,500	$15,800

GREEN HOUSE: THE ENERGY EFFICIENT HOME

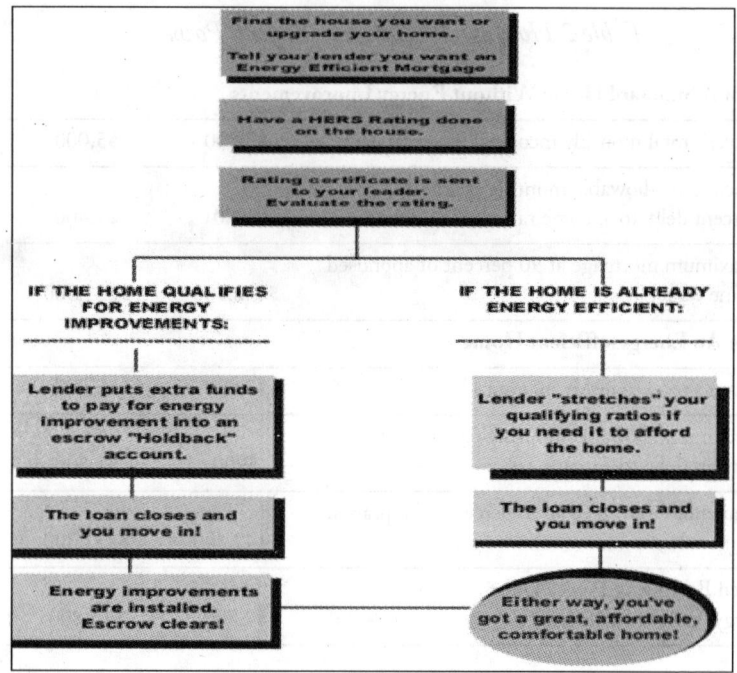

Source: Federal Citizen Information Center:
http://www.pueblo.gsa.gov/cic_text/housing/energy_mort/energy-mortgage.htm

Data on Residential Building

Size and Occupancy

A majority of Americans live in single family homes. 70% of 103 million households in the United States lived in single-family homes in 1999.

Average size of single-family and mobile homes in the US:
1955   1,170 sq. ft
1975   1,645 sq. ft
1998   2,190 sq. ft

Median square footage per person in single-family and mobile homes:
1985   633 sq. ft. per person

1993   689 sq. ft. per person
1999   713 sq. ft. per person

Average number of occupants per US household:
1975   2.9   100%
1998   2.6   a 10% decrease

Source: *"American Housing Survey"*, U.S. Bureau of Census, http://www.census.gov/

- In 1950, 9% of housing units were occupied by only one person. By 1990, this increased to 25%.

  Source: *"Historical Census of Housing Tables: Living Alone"* (2001) US Bureau of Census

- Americans spend 80 to 90% of their time indoors hence consume more energy.

  Source: *"Green Developments"* (1997), Rocky Mountain Institute

Solutions and Sustainable Alternatives

As it has been noticed that most people spend a greater portion of their time indoors, it is beneficial to reduce the operational demand of the homes. The following suggestions can significantly reduce operational energy demand:

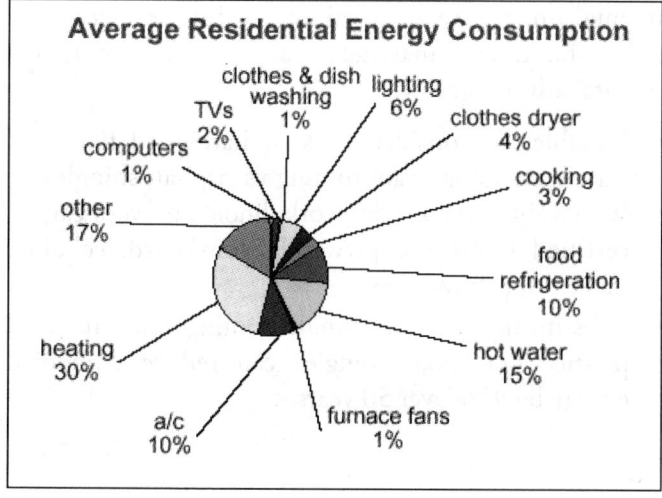

Average Residential Energy Consumption
- TVs 2%
- clothes & dish washing 1%
- lighting 6%
- clothes dryer 4%
- computers 1%
- cooking 3%
- other 17%
- food refrigeration 10%
- heating 30%
- hot water 15%
- a/c 10%
- furnace fans 1%

- Use passive heating methods such as passive solar and waste heat
- Make use of passive cooling, i.e. night-flushing and shading
- Use adequate insulation recommended R-values in the Midwest climate: attic R-50, walls R-20
- Add ceiling fans, so the A/C can be comfortably set about 5 degrees higher
- Maximize daylight- sky lights, south facing windows
- Consider decentralized, "passive" sanitary services such as compost toilet, living machine, rainwater use for toilets, grey water for gardening
- Convert appliances from electric to natural gas, reducing primary energy consumption by about 75%
- Install water-saving 2.5-gallon-per-minute showerheads ($15) to save both water and energy
- Save 40% of hot water heating energy with a simple waste-water heat exchanger

Select durable and/or renewable materials Building materials with long lives such as concrete may have greater upfront cost, but long term savings and reduced environmental impact are achieved by avoiding replacements. Renewable building materials also offer potential environmental advantages.

- Durables to consider: cork or hardwood floors vs. carpet, standing-seam roofing vs. asphalt shingles.
- Renewables to consider: cork, linoleum, wool carpet, certified wood and plywood, strawboard, cellulose insulation, straw-bale.
- Substituting asphalt shingle roofing with recycled plastic/wood fiber shingles can reduce embodied energy by 98% over 50 years.

Conclusions

Energy-efficient homes can dramatically decrease the cost of maintaining the average home. Energy-efficient homes also have the benefit of using renewable energy sources, which conserves existing energy resources.

References

Stapleton, Geoff; Milne, Geoff; and Chris Riedy: Your Home: Technical Manual- Design for Life. http://www.greenhouse.gov.au/yourhome/technical/

U.S. Department of Energy: Energy Efficiency and Renewable Energy Clearinghouse, http://www.eere.energy.gov/

U.S. Department of Energy: Energy Efficiency and Renewable Energy. Consumer Energy Information: EREC Fact Sheets, http://www.eere.energy.gov/erec/factsheets/

National Society of Professional Engineers: "Comprehensive Energy Legislation," http://www.nspe.org/govrel/gr2-4054.asp

U.S. EPA State and Local Climate Change Program: "Energy and the Home" http://yosemite.epa.gov/oar/globalwarming.nsf/UniqueKeyLookup/SHSU5BUK22/$File/energyandthehome.pdf

http://www.pueblo.gsa.gov/cic_text/housing/energy_mort/energy-mortgage.htm

http://www.kentlaw.edu/classes/fbosselm/Spring2003/student%20presentations/Energy%20efficient%20homes-Angres.ppt#18

"American Housing Survey", US Bureau of Census

"Historical Census of Housing Tables: Living Alone" (2001) US Bureau of Census

"Green Developments" (1997), Rocky Mountain Institute

Materials of Construction

Introduction

Although most houses and housing developments in North America have been in wood, use of alternate materials can save time and money and the actual construction can be easier. Many new products become available everyday and it's important that they are incorporated into building practices as they can provide a substantial benefit to both the homeowner and the builder. As these new materials become better understood they will have a significant impact on the construction industry by replacing conventional construction materials. In addition, one can include available materials in constructing the house in an innovative manner to make better use in residential applications.

It is very difficult to build an economical house entirely out of one of the building materials, including wood. Therefore, it is better to think concrete, steel or wood house as a good house material in which all components of the house need to be considered. Glover (Glover, J.) compares houses chosen from earlier study in which they are assessed with their efficiency in different ways including life cycle cost analysis. She has compared flooring, walls and the roofing using data from Buchanan and Honey, and Lawson.

Material Technologies

Structural insulated panels (SIP) have been used since 1952 and thus, the technology for these panels system is not new. SIP construction is an engineered system which provides an alternative to conventional stick-built construction methods.[21] SIP offers strength and structural performance along with

---

[21] http://www.healthgoods.com/Education/Healthy_Home_Information/Insulation/new_insulation.htm

high energy efficiency. These panels are primarily used in low-rise residential and commercial buildings as the exterior walls and roofs. These panels are generally load-bearing and use laminates of foam core and the facing is applied with an adhesive. Rigid foam cores are typically composed of either expanded polystyrene (EPS), polyurethane or polyisocyanurate and wood sheathing materials used for building the exterior walls, roof, floor and even foundations in homes and commercial buildings. Manufactured in factories, the panels are shipped to the building site and assembled. The resulting structure provides an extremely strong, well-insulated and comfortable building shell. Some 60 different companies manufacture panels throughout North America.

SIPs typically range in thickness from 4" to 12" and can be up to 24' long. Roof spans range between 12' and 14'and floors, typically up to 16'. Openings for windows and doors can be cut on the jobsite. Two structural skins give panels the necessary strength to withstand axial, bending, and racking and shear loads. They can be designed to withstand winds in excess of 160 mph and meet seismic Zone 4 requirements. SIPs have excellent thermal performance and provide significant energy saving up to 40% energy for heating and cooling home with SIP wall and ceiling panels. Structure built with SIP's looks similar to any other structure. Its strength and efficiency characteristics however are exceptional.

Use of Different Concretes

Josef Hebel developed autoclaved aerated concrete (AAC) about 1923 in Sweden in response to a timber shortage. AAC can be formed as lightweight, precast wall units made from sand, cement, lime, water, gypsum and a proprietary expansion agent. Comparable wall units weigh about one-fifth of standard concrete wall units. The constituents are mixed, poured into a form and allowed to rise. Tiny bubbles are formed throughout the AAC during the expansion process.

Once removed from the mold and cut into predetermined sizes, the unit is sent to an autoclave chamber where it is steam-cured under pressure to achieve its structural strength. One important quality of this product is its uniform cellular structure which is easy to cut with a handsaw and receives nails easily. Standard dimensions for the wall unit block are 24" long by 8" in height. Widths range from 4" to 10". Other products offered by Hebel include; wall panels, floor and roof panels, arches, staircases, lintels, and wall lintels. The system consists of small masonry-like units, larger "jumbo" units, panels, and a variety of specially manufactured shapes and pre-assembled wall sections. The walls, floors and roof of a building can be constructed with the system.

AAC is known as an environmentally friendly construction material. Compared to the energy consumed in production of many other basic building materials, only a fraction is required to produce AAC. Raw material consumption is very low for the amount of finished product produced. In the manufacturing process, no pollutants or toxic by-products are produced. AAC is also completely recyclable. Due to excellent insulation qualities of AAC, the energy consumption for the heating and cooling of buildings is greatly reduced compared to most conventional wall and roof systems. No pollutants or toxic substances are released in the finished structure that could affect indoor air quality, even in the event of fire.

The insulated reinforced masonry system (IMSI) is a block system with special cores filled with insulation inserts. These blocks may be stacked without cores, and rebar along with grout are used to reinforce the walls. Once the blocks are stacked, a surface bonding cement finishing is applied and locks the entire system together. A second coat has to be applied as a finish. Typical facings applied are elastomeric paint, regular of synthetic stucco, full or thin brick, artificial stone or siding. The IMSI System is competitive in cost with other insulated wall materials. The inserts are made from expandable polystyrene (EPS). The assembly provides a wall system capable of achieving higher thermal R values than conventional masonry and is structurally sound.

Use of Different Types of Steels in Hybrid Composite System

Steel has been the dominant commercial building material for many years. This is due to its high strength-to-weight ratio. It is produced in strict accordance with national standards and is not subject to regional inconsistencies. In addition, it will not rot, creep, warp or be damaged by termites. Steel framing has long been the method of choice in commercial buildings and high-rise structures. An increasing number of builders have discovered lightweight steel framing for constructing homes. The lightweight steel sections are typically cold-rolled and very thin and generally galvanized with protective coating. They are generally used in commercial applications; however, they can be used in residential internal walls in place of wooden sections of 2" x 4" with 2" x 4" channels. Details are shown in a later chapter with actual applications. In addition, they can be used in light gauge metal decks for supporting concrete while wet. Thus, one can create a hybrid steel-composite floor system. The main advantage of this composite system is that the floor does not need to be supported as in the conventional basement structures with steel columns interrupting the available space. In the basement of the Sabnis house, the span is over 20' and results in a clear floor space for use for large gatherings. A second advantage of the system results from the large compressive strength of concrete compared to wood. The concrete floor does not vibrate and does not easily transmit noises between floors, so walking around in the home is quieter. These floor systems are also useful where in-floor radiant heating is used. In homes with radiant heating, the heat distribution tubing is encased in the concrete, warming the entire floor. These advantages cannot be equated in actual cost savings, but give the owner a richer living quality. One of the steel-concrete composite floor types, ComFlor 46[22] was introduced in 1985, Using a simple trapezoidal composite deck it provides a strong reliable performance floor. Its profile is economic and nestable, reducing transport and handling costs. Ceilings and lightweight utility services can easily be attached to the punched hangar tabs, which can be specified and included with ComFlor 46. Concrete usage is low due to its trapezoidal profile resulting in savings in the overall costs. Typical section of such a composite floor is shown in Figure 1. The floor with deck and concrete is less than 2"; each can span up to 10'; with recycled steel beams for support it can span up to 30' and can be very economically used for large homes. Use of lightweight concrete can further reduce the floor dead load in the system.

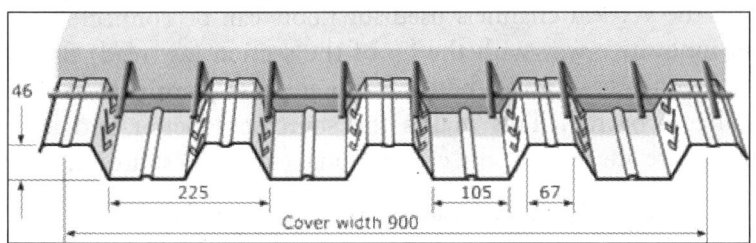

Figure1 Typical section of a composite floor

The manufacturer provides quick reference tables to estimate load/span and other details as a guide for initial design, based on the parameters stated below the tables. Slab is provided with fibermesh for shrinkage reduction (compared to reinforcing steel). Additional information may be found from the website.[23]

---

[22] http://www.coruspanelsandprofiles.co.uk/htm/comflor-46.htm
[23] http://www.coruspanelsandprofiles.co.uk/htm/comflor-fibredeck.htm

Figure 2 Steel joist composite System[24]

Another system, which uses open web light steel trusses to support deck and concrete, is shown in Figure 2. This system can also span large spaces without intermediate columns. The composite joist forming system is flexible (in design) and meets different types of construction configurations.

An application of the steel-concrete system can also be used very effectively in building staircases. The floor beams and the vertical channels used for floors can be connected in an innovative way with the lip of the section (as tread) filled with concrete to give a better finish and also sturdiness to the staircase overall. This makes the staircase a better and less expensive alternate to the conventional (squeaky) staircase.

Advantages and Disadvantages of Various Systems

Exterior insulation and finish systems (EIFS) were first introduced as commercial cladding products but have now moved into the residential market sector. EIF systems consist mainly of five components; an adhesive, insulation board, base coat on the face of insulation board, glass fiber-reinforced mesh and a finish coat, which protects the entire system. EIFS provide a complete layer of insulation, which significantly reduces air infiltration. It is capable of being used in all climates and regions. The system insulates homes in both hot and cold weather. The insulation board protects against heat flow passing into and out of the home. Thus,

---

[24] http://www.hambrosystems.com/

heat is retained in cold temperatures and blocked in hot temperatures. If installed incorrectly, moisture can become trapped between the insulation board and substrate. This can result in damage from dry rot and mildew.

Construction Techniques

With the installation of some these alternative materials, it is necessary to use the proper tools in order to achieve a quality finished product. The conventional handsaw, keyhole saw and utility knife make up some of the basic tools. For expanded polystyrene (EPS), extruded polystyrene (XPS), exterior insulation and finish systems (EIFS) products and insulting concrete forms (ICF), a hot wire cutting machine is typically faster than a handsaw. A thermal hot knife with a "V" blade can be used to cut channels for electrical wire and/or boxes. Also the hot knife can be used for cutting polystyrene.

In terms of gluing joints, it is important to choose an adhesive that is compatible with the material. In the case of polystyrene, polyurethane foam can be used as both an insulating sealant and an adhesive. It expands and assumes the shape of a cavity, forming an airtight seal. In addition, it fills holes and gaps, especially around pipes. In ICF systems, rebar is used and most often will have to be cut. Commonly, a rebar cutter-bender is used. Installation of ICF systems can be done by the individual and there is the option of using the form to build a complete wall system for an entire structure. The poured-in-place systems are also available, which use XPS foam panels. These systems have similarities to the ICF system but also provide the option to cut the ties and salvage up to 90% of the foam board.

Insulated Concrete Forms for Walls

Concrete is wet when poured and therefore needs a form until it is hardened (in 24-48 hours) and possesses its own strength.

The forms may be made of wood or steel and their use depends on availability of materials, including reuse of metal. When the form is made of foam insulation, either pre-formed interlocking blocks or separate panels connected with ties, they are known as insulated concrete forms (ICF)[25]. ICFs are basically forms for poured concrete walls, which stay in place as a permanent part of the wall assembly. The left-in-place forms not only provide a continuous insulation and sound barrier, but also a backing for drywall on the inside, and stucco, lap siding, or brick on the outside and provide significant insulating capability.

A review[26] of the history of ICFs reveals that the technology first established a strong marketplace in the late 1960s in Europe, where wood resources were at a premium and there was a strong tradition of building durable, long-lasting structures with stone and concrete. In North America, Werner Gregori applied for a Canadian patent in 1966 for a *"self-supporting concrete form of rigid, low-density foamed plastic, adapted to be left in place to provide insulation for a wall formed ... by such forms which have been filled with concrete."* He called his system *Foam Form of Canada* and received patents for his forming system in North America and several European countries later.

ICFs were developed in the United States in the 1980's, and later. ICF structures are durable and require little maintenance. They save energy and are environmentally friendly. In addition, they are very quiet and comfortable. ICF structures promote healthy indoor environments and resist warping and shrinkage when exposed to the elements during construction. Finally, they provide maximum protection from fires, storms, high winds, and other natural conditions. In 1995 there were some 20 different brands of ICF forms marketed in North America, with 4-5 new systems introduced

---

[25] http://www.forms.org/product_info/technology.html
[26] http://www.glaciernw.com/reference_article.asp?ra_id=59

annually. Today (2005) there must be close to 80 different brands/manufacturers of ICF.

All ICFs work on the same principle although the various brands differ widely in the details of their shapes, cavities and component parts. Concrete walls built with ICFs give the house superior comfort, solidity, durability, resistance to natural disasters, quietness, and energy efficiency. They offer both home buyers and home builders a superior alternative to wood frame walls.

ICF Block systems have the smallest individual units, ranging from 8" x 16" (height by length) to 16" x 4'. A typical ICF block is 10" in overall width, with a 6" cavity for the concrete. The units are factory-molded with special interlocking edges that allow them to fit together like children's plastic Lego™ blocks. Panel systems have the largest units, ranging from roughly 1' x 8', to 4' x 12'. Their foam edges are flat, and interconnection requires attachment of a separate connector or "tie." Panels are assembled into units before setting in place either on-site or by the local distributor prior to delivery.

Plank systems are similar to panel systems, but generally use smaller faces of foam, ranging in height from 8" to 12", and in width from 4' to 8'. The major difference between planks and panels is the manner of assembly. The foam planks are outfitted with ties as part of the setting sequence rather than being pre-assembled into units. Within these broad categories of ICFs individual brands vary in their cavity design. "Flat wall" systems yield a continuous thickness of concrete, like a conventional poured wall. "Grid wall" systems have a waffle pattern where the concrete is thicker at some points than others. "Post and beam" systems have widely spaced horizontal and vertical columns of concrete which are completely encapsulated in foam. Whatever the differences among ICF brands, all major ICF systems are engineer-designed, code-accepted, and field-proven.

ICF provides several advantages compared to wooden walls. They include:

Comfort: Houses built with ICF walls have a much more even temperature throughout the day and night. They have virtually no "cold spots" and draughts are sharply reduced.

Solidity: The rigidity of concrete construction reduces the flexibility in floors and reduces shifting and vibration from the force of the wind or the slamming of a door. Concrete houses survive high-force winds like hurricanes far better than wood homes. When properly reinforced, they withstand earthquakes well.

Quietness: The ICF wall is six times more effective against sound transmission compared to the ordinary frame wall. This reduces noise from outside and allows construction of houses near highways.

Energy efficiency: The superior insulation, air tightness, and mass of the external walls cut the amount of energy needed for heating and cooling by 30-40%. This can save substantially in utility costs in a typical home in the order of several hundred dollars annually. Smaller heating and cooling equipment can be used and can reduce the initial cost of a house by over one thousand dollars.

Design flexibility: ICF houses can be completed with almost any interior and exterior finishes and can take any shape as easily as wood frame. In fact, some interesting effects, such as curved walls and frequent corners, can be less expensive to build into an ICF home.

For different systems available[27] one should refer to the references cited since there are a substantial numbers of manufacturers who are willing to share information with interested parties. Some of them are mentioned later in

---

[27] http://www.forms.org/Primary%20Search/Primary%20Member%20Search.htm

Chapter 6 where model homes are included as examples of ICF and energy-efficient homes.

The ICF wall system has the potential to have the highest overall R-value of the various foundation systems and can be constructed as high as R-35. Since the forms are designed to resist the load of wet concrete, they must be relatively thick. The two layers (interior and exterior) of insulation provide the high R-value.

Since ICF systems are gaining popularity homeowners like them because they conserve energy, create a habitable space in the basement, and provide the thermal continuity for the home. Builders like them because they are easy to construct, reduce construction time, and have integral fastening strips to facilitate finishing. Modern technology has reduced the probability of toxicity, volatile organic compounds, flame spread, and smoke-spread with the latest insulated concrete form products, making them a healthy alternative for building.

Insulated Concrete Floors

Since ICF has been used for walls it makes sense to increase the construction value by using it in floors as well. In the last couple of years, insulating "stay-in-place" forms have been used for reinforced concrete floors in the house. This eliminates the steel sections shown outside, but are used in hidden form as shown in Figure 3. In addition to the main advantage of quietness between the floors, other advantages include: clear spans up to the entire length of the house (up to 40'), thereby making room arrangement flexible; a sturdy floor with insulation already in place. Internal joists are spaced 24" on centers similar to the wooden joists. In Figure 4 is shown the additional in-floor heating system that is cast into the floor, which makes the floor not only well insulated, but also warm in winter.

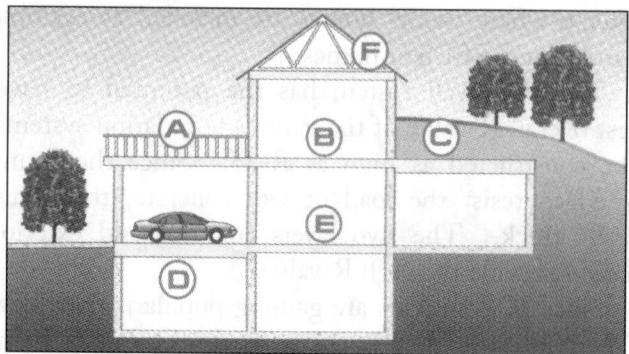

Figure 3 ICF floors can be used in various forms shown here: A: Deck and Patio; B, E: Floor; C: Earth-covered roof; D: Garage floor, and F: Ceiling

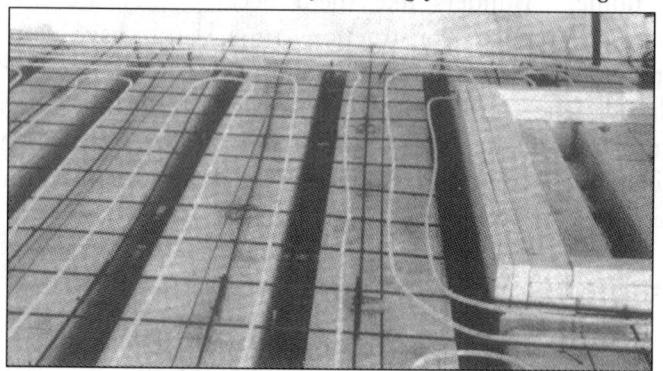

Figure 4 In-floor heating system can be cast in ICF Floor

Insulation Materials

Insulation materials play a primary role in achieving high energy efficiency in buildings. Fiberglass is considered a risk by some because of the ability of insulation fibers to become airborne and be inhaled similar to asbestos. Cellulose insulation uses recycled newsprint that contains printer's ink and can possibly outgas formaldehyde into a home. Perlite™ insulation is in a loose form suitable to fill the cavities in building block. Perlite can be bound into other materials and used in sheet form. It is commonly used in commercial roofing material and can be used as an aggregate in concrete. It is non-flammable, lightweight and chemically inert.

Cotton insulation is environmentally friendly and is made from 100% recycled materials such as cotton and other natural fibers; these fibers come from trimmings from the denim manufacturing industry, for example, and are otherwise usually dumped in landfills. A fire retardant is added to the fibers before they are combined into cotton batts.[28] The fibers do not contain formaldehyde or other chemical irritants. There are several advantages of cotton insulation: they are non toxic; transmit 10% less sound; perform better at low temperatures and in windy conditions compared to fiberglass, which can lose 35-50% of its R-value when the outdoor temperature is 70°F colder than the indoor temperature.

Other Materials Used in Residential Construction

Fiberock™ is a fiber-reinforced gypsum panel that is designed for two types of application: underlying boards and wallboard. Both applications are manufactured with cellulose fibers, obtained from recycled newspaper and are mixed with gypsum and Perlite to provide strength throughout the panel. Unlike standard gypsum wallboard, Fiberock is fabricated on an assembly line in order to create a uniform panel. Fiberock can be obtained in lengths up to 12'. Another type of Fiberock available is Fiberock VHI™ which is available in lengths up to 10'. It features fiberglass mesh reinforcements and works well in areas where very high impact (VHI) resistance is required. Both Fiberock and Fiberock VHI are fire-resistant, but aren't recommended for use as a base for tile or wall panels in wet areas.

Wallboard repair clips are a helpful remedy to repairing holes in wallboards. Sheetrock drywall repair clips are commonly used and are designed for both ½" and ¼" wallboard. These clips meet building code requirements for repairing one-hour fire-rated partitions. Flexible gypsum

---

[28] Batts are pre-cut pieces of insulation material (such as, fiberglass, recycled cotton etc.). Batts may have a facing of paper or aluminum foil, but can be without facing also.

panels create a smoothed curved surface that is aesthetically pleasing. Sheet sizes are 4' x 8' and ¼" thick. Instead of having to wet the standard panel to create the architectural design, flexible wallboard allows one to manipulate the board with much greater ease and accuracy. The flexible wallboard is made of a fire-resistant gypsum core, encased in heavy natural-finish paper.

Advantages Related to Durability, Fire Resistance and Termite Control

Concrete is strong and durable (needs much less maintenance than wood) and when used properly. In addition to durability, concrete resists fire and wind and is not prone to termite attack. Fire resistance gives houses built with ICF's certain safety advantages including potentially lower homeowner's insurance rates.

Experience has shown that concrete structures survive fire much more readily than structures built with other materials. Unlike wood, concrete does not burn; unlike steel, it does not soften and bend. Concrete does not break down until it is exposed to very high temperatures - far above the level in a typical house fire. Typical difference between fire ratings of concrete and wood are shown below in Figure 5.

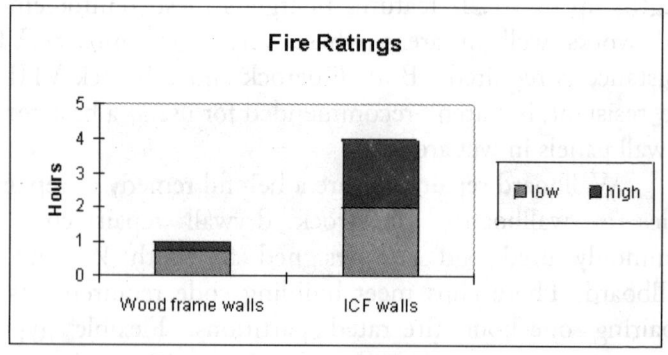

Figure 5 Fire Ratings of Wood Frame and ICF wall

Figure 5 shows that when subjected to continuous gas flames and temperatures of up to 2000°F for 4 hours, none of the ICF walls failed structurally having no significant breaks in the concrete layer. In contrast, wood frame walls typically collapse in an hour or less. Concrete walls have also proven more resistant to allowing fire to pass from one side of the wall to the other, significant in areas where brush fires are more prevalent. The test measured the passage of heat and fire from the side with the flame to the other side. The ICF walls tested did not allow flames to pass directly through or even enough heat across the wall for 2-4 hours. In contrast, wood frame walls typically allow both flame and fire-starting heat through in an hour or less.

Since the foams used in ICFs have flame-retardant additives they prevent the foams from burning by themselves. A simple test with a lit match to the material will demonstrate that it will melt away. Studies exist to indicate that fire emissions from polystyrene foams are "no more toxic" than those of wood. In short, it can be stated that ICF walls are safer in many ways than wood frame in case of a fire.

High winds, hurricanes and tornadoes present the greatest hazard to homes. They create debris and flying objects, which can penetrate and destroy homes. The residential concrete walls have a much greater impact resistance to these hazards compared to the conventionally framed walls. The tests at Texas Tech University in Lubbock, Texas successfully demonstrated that concrete walls had the strength and mass to resist the impact of wind driven debris. Debris was in the form of a 2" x4" wood stud traveling at up to 100 mph and equivalent to the weight and speed of debris generated during a tornado with 250 mph winds. This wind speed covered 99% of the tornadoes occurring in the United States.

References

Glover, J. *Which is Better? Steel, Concrete or Wood: A Comparison of Assessments on Three Building Materials in the Housing Sector*, Department of Chemical Engineering, University of Sydney, 2001

Frechette, L. A., *"Build Smarter with Alternative Materials"*, Craftsman Book Company, 1999

VanderWerf, F.C. and Munsell, *Insulating Concrete Forms Construction Manual*, McGraw-Hill Inc., New York, 1996

VanderWerf, F.C., and Lemay, L., *Insulating Concrete Forms for Residential Design and Construction*, McGraw-Hill Inc., New York, 1997.

Buchanan, A. H. and Honey, B. G, *"Energy and carbon dioxide implications of building construction"* Energy and Buildings, 1994

Lawson, W., *"Embodied Energy of Building Materials"*, The Royal Australian Institute of Architects, 1995

Concrete Homes Hotline: 1-888-333-4840 and On-line: www.concretehomes.com

http://www.boralgreen.shares.green.net.au/research3/contents.htm

http://www.healthgoods.com/Education/Healthy_Home_Information/Insulation/new_insulation.htm

http://www.forms.org

http://www.forms.org/Primary%20Search/Primary%20Member%20Search.htm

http://www.glaciernw.com/reference_article.asp?ra_id=59

http://www.ciwmb.ca.gov/publications/buyrecycled/

http://www.consumerenergycenter.org

http://www.new-technologies.org

http://www.recycle-steel.org/construction/ConClearCut.html

http://www.tfsystem.com/

http://www.ecoproducts.com/Building/build_insulation/build_cotton_insulation.htm

http://www.hambrosystems.com/

Applications of Concrete in Home Construction

Introduction

Concrete is an artificial engineering material made from a mixture of Portland cement, water, fine and coarse aggregates, and a small amount of air. It is the most widely-used construction material in the world. Concrete is the only major building material that can be delivered to the job site in a plastic state. This unique quality makes concrete desirable as a building material because it can be molded to virtually any form or shape. Concrete provides a wide latitude in surface textures and colors and can be used to construct a wide variety of structures, such as highways and streets, bridges, dams, large buildings, airport runways, irrigation structures, breakwaters, piers and docks, sidewalks, silos and farm buildings, homes, and even barges and ships.

Other desirable qualities of concrete as a building material are its strength, economy and durability. Depending on the mixture of materials used, concrete strength in compression will exceed 10,000 lb/sq in. The tensile strength of concrete is much lower, but by using properly designed steel reinforcing, structural members can be made that are as strong in tension as they are in compression. The durability of concrete is evidenced by the fact that concrete columns the Egyptians built more than 3,600 years ago are still standing.

Composition

The two major components of concrete are a cement paste and inert materials. The cement paste consists of Portland cement, water, and some air either in the form of naturally entrapped air voids or minute, intentionally entrained air bubbles. The inert materials are usually composed of fine aggregate, which is a material such as sand,

and coarse aggregate, which is a material such as gravel, crushed stone, or slag. In general, fine aggregate particles are smaller than ¼" size, and coarse aggregate particles are larger than ¼".

Depending on the thickness of the structure to be built, the size of course aggregate particles used can vary widely. In building relatively thin sections, a small size of coarse aggregate is used. At the other extreme, aggregates up to 6" or more in diameter are used in large dams. In general, the maximum size of coarse aggregates should not be larger than one-fifth of the narrowest dimensions of the concrete member in which it is used. When Portland cement is mixed with water, the compounds of the cement react to form a cementing medium. In properly mixed concrete, each particle of sand and coarse aggregate is completely surrounded and coated by this paste, and all spaces between the particles are filled with it. As the cement paste sets and hardens, it binds the aggregates into a solid mass.

Under normal conditions, concrete grows stronger as it ages. The chemical reactions between cement and water that cause the paste to harden (known as hydration) and bind the aggregates continue over time as long as 5-10 years. In the presence of moisture, concrete continues to gain strength for years. For instance, the strength of just-poured concrete may be about 1,000 lb/sq in. in one day, 4,500 lb/sq in. in 7 days, 6,000 lb/sq in. in 28 days, and 8,500 lb/sq in after 5 years.

Concrete mixtures are usually specified in terms of the dry-volume ratios of cement, sand, and coarse aggregates used. A 1:2:3 mixture for instance, consists of one part by volume of cement, two parts of sand, and three parts of coarse aggregate. Depending on the applications, the proportions of the ingredients in the concrete can be altered to produce specific changes in its properties, particularly strength and durability. The ratios can vary from 1:2:3 to 1:2:4 and 1:3:5. For high-strength concrete, the water content is kept low, with just enough water added to the entire mixture workable.

In general, more the water in concrete mix, the easier it is to work with, but it results in a weaker the hardened concrete.
Concrete can be made to have any degree of water tightness. It can be made to hold water and resist the penetration of wind-driven rains. On the other hand, for purposes such as constructing filter beds, concrete can be made porous and highly permeable. Concrete can also be given a polished surface that is as smooth as glass. By using heavy aggregates, including steel fragments, dense concrete mixtures can be made that weigh 250 lb/cu ft or more. Concrete that weighs only 30 lb/cu ft can be made by using special lightweight aggregates and foaming techniques. Forms consisting of such lightweight aggregates can be floated on water, sawed into pieces, or nailed to another surface.

After exposed surfaces of concrete have hardened sufficiently to resist marring, they should be cured by sprinkling or ponding with water or by using moisture-retaining materials such as waterproof paper, plastic sheets, wet burlap, or sand. Special curing sprays are available. The longer concrete is kept moist, the stronger and more durable it will become. In hot weather, it should be kept moist for at least three days. In cold weather, drying concrete must not be allowed to freeze. This can be accomplished by covering the cement with a tarpaulin or some other material that helps trap the heat generated by the chemical reactions within the concrete that cause it to harden.

For small jobs and minor repairs, concrete can be mixed by hand, but machine mixing endures more uniform batches and, therefore, superior performance. For most home repairs and improvements—for example, floors, walks, driveways, patios, and garden pools—the recommended proportion is a 1:2:3 mix.

Construction Technique

Concrete is poured into place in a number of ways. For the footings of small buildings, the wet concrete is poured directly into trenches dug into the earth below frost level. Concrete for foundations and certain types of walls is placed between supporting wood or metal forms, which are removed after the concrete has hardened. In lift-slab construction, floors and roof slabs are cast at ground level and then raised by hydraulic jacks and fastened to columns at the desired elevation. Slip forms are used to produce vertical shafts for silos and the cores of buildings. They are moved upward at a rate of 6 - 15 in per hour while concrete and reinforcements are put in place. The tilt-up method of construction is frequently used for one- and two-story buildings. Walls are cast in place on the ground or on the previously laid concrete floor and tilted into position by cranes. The walls are joined at the corners or between panels with cast-in-place concrete columns. To pave a highway or road with concrete, a slip-form paver is used. Two metal side forms are connected to a slip-form paver. A layer of concrete is poured between the side forms as the paver slowly moves forward on its treads; the side forms keep the concrete in position as it dries. Slip-form pavers can lay continuous strips of one or two lanes of concrete pavement.

    For certain applications, such as the construction of swimming pools, canal linings, and curved surfaces, concrete may be applied by the shotcrete method. In shotcreting, concrete is sprayed under pneumatic pressure rather than placed between forms. Often the use of shotcrete eliminates the need for formwork and permits placement of concrete in confined areas where conventional forms would be difficult or impossible to construct.

    Air-entrained concrete consists of minute air bubbles that are introduced by the addition of an admixture to the cement, either during its manufacture or during the batching and mixing of the concrete. The presence of a properly distributed amount of these bubbles imparts desirable properties to both freshly mixed and hardened concrete. In freshly mixed concrete, entrained air acts as a lubricant, improving the workability of the mix, thereby reducing the amount of water that needs to be added. Entrained air also reduces the need for fine material, such as sand. Entrained air in hardened concrete dramatically reduces the scaling that might otherwise result from the use of chemicals to melt ice on roads and streets. It also prevents damage to pavements caused by freezing and thawing. The air bubbles function as minute safety valves by providing room for the free water in concrete to expand harmlessly as freezing occurs.

Reinforced Concrete

Concrete used in most construction work is reinforced with steel. When concrete structural members must resist extreme tensile stresses, steel supplies the necessary strength. Steel is embedded in the concrete in the form of mesh, or reinforcement or twisted bars. A bond forms between the steel and the concrete, and stresses can be transferred between both components.

Concrete in Staircase

Analysis of staircases demonstrates the creativity with which architects and engineers consistently develop new combinations of structural systems and materials. This is even more astounding as relatively few fundamental structural systems exists for stairs. The elements that comprise a stair are the steps, supports, landings and the railing. Timber, concrete and steel are the first material choices for a structural system.

Two structural systems form the basis for the construction of load-bearing steps: the single span and the cantilevered support. If the single span steps are simply supported on the strings, they must act as a lateral bracing and carry the horizontal loads from the railing. However, it is also possible to weld the steps to the strings, so as to build a load bearing unit. Cantilevered steps are either rigidly fixed to a torsion resistant beam or are mechanically interlocked to the wall.

In the early days of concrete technology, such a new material was not considered as efficient in staircases. With the technologically complex formwork production of in-situ concrete, stairway elements were prefabricated and constructed in the factory. For the use of industrially manufactured pre-cast concrete elements in structural engineering, efficient transport and lifting vehicles are a prerequisite. Concrete is an economical alternative for primary and secondary staircases that complies with building regulations, because of the favorable fire resistance characteristics. The solid construction in concrete has the additional advantage that sound transmission becomes a minor problem.

While the chosen flooring can be laid directly on the stair flights, the concrete landings must still be constructed with finishing floor. If the landing is included in the prefabrication, the supports and the wall connections must be acoustically separated. Along with the extensive experiments in formwork techniques, the concrete's coloring with various aggregates and surface treatments should be examined closely, since it is common to finish prefabricated concrete stair elements with timber or stone.

Driveways[29]

In order to provide quality installation of a concrete driveway the following is recommended: concrete must be cast on a prepared sub-grade that is uniform in soil composition and compaction; for drainage, the grade must be sloped a minimum of 1/8 in. per foot from all existing structures; formwork should be securely staked providing a minimum slab depth of four inches; and both the sub-grade and formwork should be watered-down lightly prior to concrete placement. The concrete mix design should have a compressive strength of 4,000 lb/sq in. minimum at 28 days,

---

[29] http://www.concretenetwork.com/

air content of 6.5 ± 1.5%, water/cement ratio of 0.50, coarse aggregates meeting proper classification and a slump of 4 inch ± 1 inch. The higher denser concrete with typical strength of 2,500 lb/sq in provides better wear and tear.

Concrete can be affected from the moisture under the slab, and sometimes salts from the soil can leave efflorescence on the surface. The reduced water in concrete mixture provides a reduction in this wicking action. Excess water should never be added at the site, which will increase the water/cement ratio. Durable wearing surface is created with the proper sequence of placing and finishing concrete as follows: screeding or striking-off, floating then waiting for the water sheen to dissipate, followed by edging, jointing and brooming to provide a non-slip surface. Discharge from the mixer must be completed within 90 minutes of concrete batching. Prolonged mixing or delayed placement will adversely affect the quality of the concrete with regard to air content and compressive strength.

Control joints must be spaced at intervals not exceeding 10 feet with a minimum depth of cut equal to ¼ the slab thickness with centerline control joint in driveways greater than 12 feet wide. Also where new construction abuts existing structures, such as garage floors or fence posts, an isolation joint extending the full depth of the concrete slab should be provided. Finally, the driveway must be cured to attain the strength and durability potential of the concrete following its placement. In warm to mild weather climates, cure the concrete incorporating one of the following methods:

1. Applying a membrane-curing compound according to the manufacturers' instructions
2. Soaking seven-day continuous water curing
3. Saturated burlap with polyethylene cover secured in place

Often it is beneficial to employ a waterproof cover, such as insulating blankets, which maintain the curing temperature above 55°F for a minimum of seven days in colder conditions. In cold climates, air entrainment is added to the concrete at the batch plant; it allows any moisture that may enter concrete to expand in the microscopic air bubbles during freeze/thaw cycles relieving internal pressure. Reinforcement can be with either wire mesh or steel bars placed in a grid pattern at proper location. This is done using spacers to maintain the reinforcement location in the center. The reinforcement or fibers do not eliminate cracks, but simply reduce them or hold them together.

Typical Concrete Driveway[30]

Garage and Basement Slabs

Twenty years ago, standard concrete masonry block and cast-in-place concrete basement foundation wall systems were the standard for low-rise, single-family homes. Today, new products are becoming more available such as insulated concrete and encapsulated forms. The most basic foundation system is the un-insulated concrete foundation. It is helpful to use it as a basis for comparison with other systems discussed in this book.

---

[30] http://www.concretenetwork.com/concrete/concrete_driveways/index.html

Typical Basement Wall[31]

Standard Un-insulated Concrete

This system consists of a concrete strip footing on which a wall is constructed. The wall may be either concrete block or cast-in-place concrete as seen in Figure 1. Coating of Portland cement and sand is put on the exterior of the wall and a damp proof coating is applied above and below grade, along with a drain around the perimeter of the wall, embedded in graded gravel. Anchor bolts are attached to the wall to secure for the sill plate. The foundation wall can be reinforced with rebar cast into the concrete, especially where seismic load is concerned. The thermal mass of the block-work contributes little to the wall's R-value because the wall is un-insulated also soil provides limited insulation and thermal benefits.

---

[31] http://www.concretenetwork.com/featured_contractor/jlpouredwalls.htm

GREEN HOUSE: THE ENERGY EFFICIENT HOME

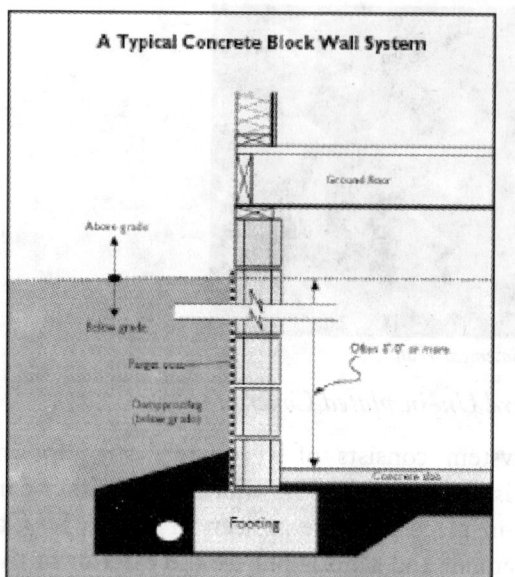

Figure 1 Typical Un-insulated Concrete Block Wall

Semi-finished Concrete Block

Better insulation is provided by the semi-finished concrete wall system shown in Figure 2. It uses the same techniques as the un-insulated concrete wall system, but insulation and drywall without tape or paint are added to the interior of the wall, making the basement potentially habitable. The additional 2"x4" wood-frame (as a false wall) is built onto the inside of the block wall. With fiberglass batt insulation between the block walls, the false wall is then covered with a 6-mil polyethylene vapor retarder and a ½", un-taped, gypsum wallboard. The R-value for this wall system is R-14. With the insulation on the interior side of the wall, the surface temperature of the drywall is relatively warm. The advantage of this foundation system is that it makes for a cleaner, brighter space that is easily finished and for homeowner the potential extra living space.

Pouring concrete into walls that have been formed with plywood or steel is one of the most economical ways to construct a basement wall. The walls are relatively easy to erect, cast, and strip. This type of system tends to be the preferred choice of builders who have access to ready-mixed concrete, chutes, slings, conveyors, or pumps.

A solid concrete wall is less permeable to air, water, and water vapor than concrete block, but solid concrete also shrinks, and shrinkage may cause cracks due to lateral loads and settlement. As this occurs, the walls need to be damp-proofed or water proofed as needed. An 8-inch solid wall has a thermal mass of about 21 Btu/sq ft/°F and has a four-hour fire rating with zero flame and smoke spread.

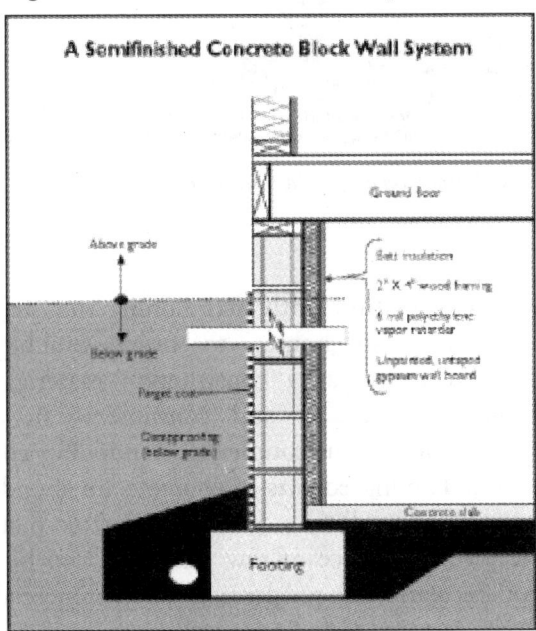

Figure 2 Semi-finished Concrete Wall

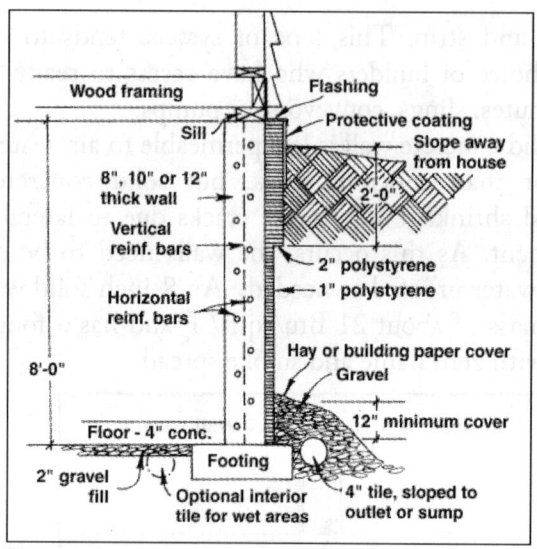

Figure 3 Components of a well-constructed concrete basement

Conclusions

Overall, concrete is in tune with maintaining the quality of the environment. From homes to office buildings to highways, using concrete as a construction material helps protect our natural resources and consumers can realize unique benefits. From an environmental standpoint, concrete has a lot to offer. The ingredients of concrete are abundant in supply and take a lesser toll than other construction materials. Quarries, the primary source of raw materials, can be easily reclaimed for recreational, residential, or commercial use. They can also be restored to their natural state.

As a nearly inert material, concrete is an ideal medium for recycling waste or industrial byproducts. Many materials that would end up in landfills instead can be used to make concrete. Blast furnace slag, recycled polystyrene, and fly ash are among materials that can be included in the recipe for concrete and further enhance its appeal. Waste products such as scrap tires and kiln dust are used to fuel the manufacture of cement. Moreover, even old concrete itself can be reborn as aggregate for new concrete mixtures.

Another environmental plus for concrete is energy efficiency. From manufacture to transport to construction, concrete is modest in its energy needs and generous in its payback. The only energy intensive demand is in the manufacture of Portland cement, which typically is 10 to 15% of the concrete component. Since the materials for concrete are so readily available, concrete products and ready-mixed concrete can be made from local resources and processed near a job site. Local shipping minimizes fuel requirements for handling and transportation.

Once in place, concrete offers significant energy savings over the lifetime of a building, a home or a pavement. Concrete's thermal mass, bolstered by insulating materials affords high R-factors and moderates temperature swings by storing and releasing energy needed for heating and cooling. In addition, the light reflective nature of concrete makes it less costly to illuminate.

Further characteristics of concrete are waste minimization and long life, whether cast-in-place or pre-cast, concrete is used on an as-needed basis. Leftovers are easily reused or recycled. Concrete is a durable material that actually gains strength over time, conserving resources by reducing maintenance and reconstruction. As a reliable and versatile product for centuries, concrete paves the way toward an environmentally secure future for generations to come.

References

Herbermann, K. J., "Staircases: Design and Construction", Basel, Boston: Birkhäuser, 2003

Concrete Network (2003), Concrete Driveway; http://www.concretenetwork.com

http://www.concretenetwork.com/concrete/concrete_driveways/index.html

GREEN HOUSE: THE ENERGY EFFICIENT HOME

Concrete Network (2003), Concrete Homes [Online], http://www.concretehomes.com

Concrete in Residential Construction (1975), Addison, Ill: Concrete Construction Publications.

http://www.concretenetwork.com/featured_contractor/jlpouredwalls.html

Case Studies of Energy-Efficient Concrete Homes

Introduction

Concrete is a material made from a mixture of cement, water, fine and coarse particles, and a small amount of air. When cement is mixed with water, the compounds of the cement react and harden. As the cement hardens, it binds the particles into a solid mass. Under normal conditions, concrete grows stronger as it becomes older. Concrete as a material can be altered to produce specific changes in its properties, particularly strength and durability. It can be made either watertight or permeable. Various mixtures of the components can produce a heavy or light concrete, which can float on water. Concrete in most construction work is reinforced with steel to compensate its weakness in tension. When concrete structural members must resist forces to cause tension, steel supplies the necessary strength. It is the most widely used construction material in the world including building decorative homes. Concrete homes especially with proper insulation are energy efficient, resistant to strong winds, practically soundproof and offer a broad range of design options.

Concrete homes offer a variety of benefits over standard construction such as:

1. Construction using insulated concrete forms (ICF) results in a faster and more efficient building cycle.
2. Versatile and Compatible Stucco, wood siding, vinyl siding, brick and other traditional exterior finishes can be easily used with ICF easier than the conventional construction.
3. Environmentally responsible concrete and polystyrene foam are inert and can be recycled.

4. Energy efficient energy savings are built in such concrete homes. Many concrete homeowners report energy savings of up to 40% or more.
5. Neither concrete nor polystyrene will rot, rust or corrode.
6. Concrete home built with ICF has much greater noise reduction characteristics than wood or steel.
7. Internationally proven throughout the world, concrete is one of the most popular forms of housing construction.

ICF construction has and can make a big impact on building better homes for us in the future. It is in the national interest to provide better future for our children and future generations. It is also good for personal, social, economical, environmental reasons and from also good engineering perspectives. An ICF home does not look any different than the conventional one, but has several advantages demonstrated in this book. One typical ICF home is shown below:

(Courtesy: www.litedeck.com)

In the following section an overview of concrete construction in housing is provided followed by several examples around the country and even some parts of developing world to illustrate these points.

Overview of Constructing Concrete Home[1]

The details of construction are directly reproduced from the site, which is referenced and again indicated in the Reference section at the end of the chapter. The reader is referred to that site for additional information.

Cast-in-place concrete homes can be built using three methods: A) Exterior Walls, B) Exterior and Interior Walls, or C) Exterior/Interior Walls and Ceiling/Floor Construction. These methods allow a builder to create a high-quality home that's safe, secure, comfortable, attractive, energy efficient and environmentally friendly.

Wall Forms

A) Exterior Walls

B) Exterior and Interior Walls

Deck Forms   Ready-to-Pour   Tunnel forms
(ceiling or floor)

C) Exterior/Interior Walls and Ceiling/Floor Construction

After creating a reinforced concrete slab foundation for the home, aluminum forms (8-foot plus tall) are erected creating 4-inch reinforced concrete walls and 6-inch concrete ceilings/floors. Tunnel forms cast walls and slabs at the same time. Electrical boxes, conduit, plumbing, and mechanical sleeves are cast-in-place to allow for future flexibility.

Pouring Concrete

Concrete is poured into the wall and deck forms. In just one day, the reinforced concrete is sufficiently cured and forms are removed. Work begins on the second level of a two-story structure. Walls, ceilings, and stairs are poured monolithically.

Removing Forms

Forms are removed from the concrete structure.

Exterior and Roof

The exterior can be finished with stucco, brick, siding, or other materials. The roof is conventionally framed of lumber or steel atop the concrete deck that forms the first or second level's roof. This allows architectural flexibility in roof design while keeping the wood or steel used for the roof framing outside of the home's fire-resistant thermal concrete envelope.

Finishing

The finished interior concrete walls and ceilings are so flat and smooth, drywall is not needed. Walls and ceilings are finished. Optional concrete crown molding available.

The Finished Product

This is the system that professional concrete forming contractors use to complete a beautiful new cast-in-place concrete-built home.

Case Studies of Concrete Homes

This section presents a number of cases in which ICF was used very effectively to construct concrete homes. They demonstrate that they are not only energy-efficient, but also have other qualities mentioned earlier in this chapter. These house illustrations were picked from various sources including the authors' own experiences. The acknowledgement is also provided to the sources, including available website, so that the reader may be able to go to the source directly. The cases come from various states in the US and Canada as well as other countries, where the cheaper labor can be utilized effectively along with concrete and ICF. Versatility of the materials and their applications are very encouraging.

Case study 1: Ohio

Martin Home in Huntsburg, Ohio

(Courtesy: www.creativebuildingproducts.com)

The Martin house shown in the views above is a hybrid concrete house. The basement and exterior walls are poured ICF concrete, and the inside walls are conventional wooden construction. The house is 1,500 sq ft with a finished basement of the same size. The ceiling is R32. The propane tank is the smallest (300 gallons) that our provider could install and we were warned that it would not be sufficient. The yearly use for the past three winters has been about 450 gallons and we are charged a penalty each year for under-utilization of propane for heating. Regulation of propane suppliers against penalty charges would assist new owners in the area to maintain even lower heating bills and confirm the energy efficiency of the construction technique. The fireplace is also fired with propane and although wood from the obviously heavily wooded lot is burned, propane is used for start-up and often for burning on its own.

The lot is in the Lake Erie snow-belt, east of Cleveland, with approximately 150 inches of snow fall during the season, and the average annual temperature is reportedly about 0.5°F lower than Anchorage Alaska. The driveway, apron and the back patio areas are also concrete. The home is on a quiet area but we can't even hear the snowplow in the driveway. My wife enjoys the deep window sills afforded by the width of the ICF and the 8 inch poured concrete walls, on which she places plants, seasonal decorations and ceramics.

Case studies 2-3: Virginia

Two ICF Homes in Henrico County, Virginia

Courtesy: http://www.creativebuildingproducts.com

This house has a finished area of 3,500 sq. ft. located in Virginia and is all electric with a heat pump of 3½ T capacity with four thermostats. Like most houses built with insulated concrete forms, this house has no foundation vents; but the crawl space has been conditioned to maintain at the same temperature as the rest of the house. These conditioned crawl spaces do not support the growth of mold and mildew, both of which are major sources of allergens. They also reduce air infiltration into the home resulting in no drafts and any cold spots especially along the floor. Conditioned crawl space provides more comfortable environment with lower energy bills. A record of this home's utility bill over a period of five years (1994-99) averaged monthly electric bill of approximately $140 per month; this is comparable to $300 of this type and size house in the area.

(Courtesy: www.creativebuildingproducts.com)

The second house shown above is located in Henrico County, Virginia and is all electric with a finished area of over 4,000 sq. ft. It has a single 3½ T unit with five thermostats. The exterior walls of this house were constructed with insulated concrete form (ICF) and reinforced with steel reinforcement. This combination provides superior protection against winds in excess of 200 miles per hour. ICF walls have proved to be very sound proof, a nice feature for those who plan to build in a crowded neighborhood or along a busy street. Another feature of ICF walls is their ability to insulate well, to make the house with comfortable environment and reduced electric bills.

Case study 4: Texas

NAHB Show Case Home, 2000

This 3,474 sq. ft in Heath, Texas[32] was built by Marshall Bobbitt Homes and the Portland Cement Association (PCA) as part of their promotion of concrete homes during the annual International Builders' Show, sponsored by the National Association of Home Builders January 14–17 in 2000. Located adjacent to a golf course in the Buffalo Creek subdivision, the 3,474-square-foot home is one of several to be built in the development using **insulating concrete forms** (ICF) for the exterior walls. Research shows that most builders believe homebuyers will be willing to pay 2% to 5% more than wood framing for the quality of a concrete home. According to the builder, "There are a lot of advantages to having a concrete home. Benefits like pest resistance and soundproofing, energy efficiency, balanced with the strength of concrete walls for safety, add to the value of the house."

---

[32] http://www.cement.org/homes/ch_showhomes.asp

Case Study 5: Atlanta, Georgia[33]

The nearly 6,000 square foot home in the prestigious Buckhead area of Atlanta was designed by the prominent Atlanta architects Harrison Design Associates and constructed by Benecki Builders, Ltd. Polysteel Southeast were the contractors for the ICF walls and safe room. The Portland Cement Association (PCA) sponsored this concrete show home at the International Builders Show in Atlanta. The home has incorporated a number of concrete products, including insulating concrete form (ICF) exterior walls, an ICF safe room, a structural hollow-core floor system, decorative flatwork, concrete retaining walls, and a Portland cement stucco exterior finish. The concrete for the project was provided by Blue Circle Materials and Thomas Concrete.

---

[33]http://www.cement.org/homes/ch_showhomes.asp

GREEN HOUSE: THE ENERGY EFFICIENT HOME

Case Study 6: Homestead, Florida[34]

The conventional concrete home shown above is from Homestead, FL. It was built by Secure Structures, Inc. to prove that homes can be built to withstand the thrashings given by hurricanes. It is a 2,600 square foot modest three bedroom, two-car garage home and includes a family room, kitchen, dining room, and three bathrooms. The foundation, walls and even the roof of the home are all made of concrete that was poured on site.

The house was built with in-place-concrete using pump to make the construction faster and economical. The roof concrete contains a waterproofing agent to help protect the roof against the heavy rains that come with hurricanes and polypropylene fibers in all the concrete mixtures used to minimize shrinkage and early cracking.

A number of advantages must be cited here. Computer simulation showed that this home could withstand wind speeds of up to 600 mph, considerably more than the speed ever recorded during any tornado or hurricanes. Tightly sealed concrete also prevents the exchange of air through the

---

[34]http://www.personal.psu.edu/users/d/j/djf164/classwork/CE436/Homestead/Homestead.html

unintentional passages, such as connections, is minimized to keep out the irritating airborne particles such as pollen, dust, and vehicle exhaust. On the other hand, fresh air cannot come through the concrete and the inside air may become stale; this may necessitate the home to have air exchanger. Concrete is also a very thermally efficient material and therefore keeps home cooler in the summer and warmer in the winter. This leads to significant savings on energy costs as compared to other building materials such as wood. This advantage will be desirable in all climates. Several other advantages are indicated in many other examples.

GREEN HOUSE: THE ENERGY EFFICIENT HOME

Case Study 7: ICF Home in Nevada[35]

The New American Home in Las Vegas, Nevada[36]

The New American Home (TNAH) was an annual showcase project in Las Vegas, Nevada in 2004. It was sponsored in part by the National Association of Home Builder's National Council of the Housing Industry. The Energy Star® home shown above reveals a modern "loft" design, concrete providing the vast majority of the structural elements. The visible and invisible benefits of concrete give life to a refreshing demonstration of new ideas for designing, living,

---

[35] http://www.cement.org/homes/ch_sh_tnah04.asp
[36] http://www.concretehomes.com; www.tnah.com

and building. The 5,180 sq. ft. home demonstrates an excellent use of natural light and building materials. Insulating concrete forms (ICFs) make up the high performance envelope for the below- and above-grade walls. Three different concrete flooring techniques, integrated with decorative finishing, appear on all three levels, as well as the exterior decks. The exterior finish features decorative concrete masonry and stucco with exposed masonry functioning as a beautiful interior wall finish.

The home was designed to reach a *Home Energy Rating System* (HERS) score of 90 (above the current Energy Star rating requirement of 86), thanks to a high performance technologies including ICFs. ICF exterior walls offer greater energy efficiency, improved comfort through less air infiltration and reduced sound penetration, and greater strength and durability - without sacrificing beauty and architectural flexibility. The house will use 46 percent less energy for space heating and cooling, hot water, and lighting than a standard home.

Case Study 8: ICF in Myrtle Beach, South Carolina[37]

An ICF Home in Myrtle Beach, SC

ICF construction is made a major impact in the homebuilding industry in Myrtle Beach, South Carolina. The community has more than 200 ICF homes built since 1999, which gives Myrtle Beach one of the highest concentrations of ICF homes in the country. This includes the prestigious Grande Dunes development with over 100 luxury ICF homes have been built. The greater Myrtle Beach area, known as "The Grand Strand" for its world-class beaches golf courses, and resorts, is well suited to ICF construction with its location between the Atlantic Ocean and the Intra-coastal Waterway being *very vulnerable to hurricanes.* In addition the homeowners enjoy other advantages of energy efficiency, quietness, and termite resistance of the ICF wall system.

---

[37] http://www.cement.org/homes/ch_newsletter2004-11&12.asp#Beach

Case Study 9: Application of ICF in Moderately Priced Homes[38]

One of ICF homes in Carpentersville, Illinois

The ICF homes can also make an impact in the community by constructing them in moderately priced neighborhood. An example is cited about the economically depressed suburb of Chicago Heights, which had a number of vacant lots with delinquent taxes in 2001. In response, Chicago Heights made these lots available to builders and developers interested in constructing new, affordable housing. Advantage of using ICF construction was taken as a challenge by Energy Block, Inc and Cardenas Builders.

The energy efficiency and durability of ICF construction were major factors for gaining the support of Chicago Heights municipal officials. Continually rising energy prices, ongoing noise problems near O'Hare, and an increasing emphasis on providing economically depressed areas with affordable, quality housing ensured the increased awareness and usage of ICFs for residential construction. This

---

[38] http://www.cement.org/homes/newsletter/2001/ch_NL05_May2001.pdf

approach has provided the industry a needed push in the Chicago area over the last few years and hopefully it will be looked favorably by the administrations in other cities with similar areas, such as Washington, DC, Philadelphia, New York City to mention just a few.

Below are a few pictures of concrete homes around the world.

Case study 10: West Indies

Concrete homes have been very popular in St. Vincent. Similar to most other homes in this area, concrete was the material of choice in building this house because it protects well against the high exposure of hurricanes and termites in the area. The construction of this home had many setbacks, not normally encountered in US construction practice, but the people on the island of Mustique in West Indies found way to make the local efforts work.

Social Aspect: Most of the laborers were not adequately educated and therefore did not understand various technologies or follow the standards and codes. Even with a limited availability of machinery and only limited understanding of working of concrete, these natives often have produced the desired final product. Furthermore, they probably did not even have access to the proper materials for their proper use.

Material Constraints: The biggest problem in the island was availability of very few ways of importing essential materials onto the island in an economical way. Therefore, the use of local existing materials on the island is always desirable. The aggregate in the island is typically very coarse sand. The size of the aggregate ranges from fine sand to large chunks of stone of diameter of one inch or greater. Also, mixing proper water was another challenge. The island of Mustique has very limited fresh water supply, so the water used on this project was a combination of collected rainwater and contaminated with salt water. The coarse sand had smaller load bearing capacity than the expected standard.

Handling and Mixing of Material: When the aggregate is delivered, it is dumped directly onto the ground where it mixes with dirt and pieces of plants. The water is usually delivered in dump trucks or wheelbarrows. Even if the water collected was potable at one time, by the time it gets to the jobsite, it is dirty and unacceptable by United States standards. Once the aggregate and water are brought to the jobsite they are usually mixed in wooden boxes, wheelbarrows, or sometimes one cubic-yard mixers. These mixing containers are rarely cleaned properly and old crusted concrete particles work there way into the new mix. Another handling problem relates to reinforcing steel. On the jobsite, the contractors did not know if the milling number on the bars were according to British or American standards. Since the bars are all imported to Mustique, they usually are drenched in saltwater during the trip because they are stored openly on the ship's deck.

The concrete is mixed in such small batches, the biggest being a 1-cubic-yard-mixer (Refer to Fig. 2); therefore, testing of the concrete becomes pointless. Most of the concrete poured to make this house was carried bucket by bucket from the nearby area where it was mixed. It would be nearly impossible to test all of the mixed batches for slump and strength. Cube tests are sometimes used to test the concrete strength, but sometimes those tests are unreliable. The cubes are cured properly in a water bath. However, the concrete on the jobsite could possibly be wet down and then sacs of cement are thrown on top of it to hold in moisture. These poor curing techniques prevent the concrete from reaching its expected strength. This factor causes several problems with the formwork (Refer to Fig. 1). Being no stranger to strong winds and storms, it is a mystery how the homes in Mustique can overcome these natural weather patterns even with such poor use of materials in the building process.

Fig. 1: Framework of concrete house in St. Vincent
Source: *http://www.personal.psu.edu/users/d/j/djf164/classwork/CE436/ WestIndies/Formwork/Formwork.html*

Fig. 2: 1 cubic-yard mixer
Source: http://www.personal.psu.edu/users/d/j/djf164/classwork/CE436/WestIndies/Mixer/Mixer.html

Some Examples of Concrete Homes around the World

Homes in Bolivia[39]

In 1994, Western Forms built new concrete homes in Cochabamba, Bolivia. There were 1200 units, which were built by Tomsco shown below.

---

[39] http://www.westernforms.com/apps/conhomes/conhomesdom.shtml

Housing Developments in Santiago, Chile[40]

Western Forms built two concrete housing developments: "Santa Marta and El Carmen Huechurba" in Santiago, Chile with the cooperation by Constructora Concreta in Santiago, Chile. These projects included the development of 400 units.

---

[40] http://www.westernforms.com/apps/conhomes/conhomesdom.shtml

Single-family concrete homes were built in Merida, Yucatan, Mexico[41]

New single-family concrete homes were built in Merida, Yucatan, Mexico. During 1995, Western Forms were used in the 1000-unit block.

Conclusions

Although the use of concrete in the construction of homes is popular through out the world, it is not as popular as in the United States. As the case studies have shown concrete is a very resilient and versatile material and it is ideal for unconventional functions. Along with amazing durability, these homes offer wonderful insulation, fairly economical and resist termites.

There are few possible reasons concrete homes are not as popular as in the U.S. One such reason is contractors and civil engineers who specialize in concrete design would rather build and design large commercial structures. A second reason is even if a contractor decided to initiate major concrete construction of homes; the chances of getting a loan to start the job are slim to none. Banks, along with other financial institutions are afraid of the unknown, and they

---

[41]http://www.westernforms.com/apps/conhomes/conhomesdom.shtml

often hesitate to loan money to a non-standard construction practice. And third, very few homebuyers in the U.S. are aware that concrete homes can even be constructed and those who are aware of the fact, often think that the homes will be colorless and very boring.

References

http://www.ConcreteNetwork.com (2003); Building a Home with Concrete [On-line]:
http://www.concretenetwork.com/concrete/homes/index.html
Construction Home Council/Construction Process [On-line]:
http://www.concretehomescouncil.org/b_developers/c_process.html
Flasco, Brandon. Concrete Home Construction: A Case Study Comparing Practices in the West Indies to those in the United States [Online]:
http://www.personal.psu.edu/users/d/j/djf164/classwork/CE436/CE436project.html
Wisconsin Ready Mixed Concrete Association, Concrete Homes an Idea Whose Time Has Come [On-line]: http://www.wrmca.com/chomes.html

Building Your Own Composite Concrete Home

Introduction

Building a home is always an experience. I was educated in civil engineering and became appreciative of problems in housing with my own experience of more than three decades, but was still a novice in the business of constructing "Our Own Home". I learned a lot more through this project and want to present the whole process in this chapter, so that it makes an impact on the construction industry and the many individuals, who may look for opportunities like us to build their house, but not have to face the similar problems. This particular chapter is full of construction pictures with our own experiences, which will give an A-Z story as well as a better perspective of home building.

Planning

Our planning started in terms of our own requirements. It started with a thought to expand our 17 year old home by adding more room. Once we found out that these modifications would cost much more than our expectations, this thinking phase ended quickly. Then came the idea of a new home and everyone in the family got excited and involved, including children. We considered how every one viewed his/her part in the house and what came out was interesting! Our dream house became so big and with many amenities we just could not afford. We had bought a modest ½ acre wooded lot with trees being our requirement in the property. Trees bring a much more natural living and age-old perspective of living with the nature without leaving home or looking to spend time away from home on the week-ends. It is true that in the case of high winds, the trees may fall and cause damage to the house but such hazards exist. Thus, we made our own plans, but as every home owner in the world, we were anxious to find out how our house would look when finally finished. Both libraries and book-stores had many books, which showed plans and perspectives, which attracted our attention; some of these books offered to provide the whole set of plans for one to go about building a house. In 1995, the cost of these plans (in a totally finished form was a mere $495); so, we got a set of these drawings. Today, these drawings have been replaced with software and are very useful for a prospective homeowner. These drawings helped us to see the final look of the house, but with the software you could really build your own custom home by changing some dimensions and the process is not complicated at all. We changed some sizes of rooms to make them acceptable and we were well on our way to build our own home.

Budgeting

There is really no myth about this. However, one needs to make a decision on how much to spend on the house. For someone who owns a home already has equity and owning property always helps. This means that the budget is only for the new house or to insure that one would not go beyond his own financial capabilities and not get stuck later with financing charges. Fortunately, we are lucky to have the banks and mortgage lenders in the United States who are very cooperative (to generate their own business, but still help the borrower). In our case, we owned land with a free and clear title, which was a good beginning; the bank gave us a bridge loan to construct a home and enough time to sell our old home to move in to the new one without any problem for again borrowing the money. Thus, for budget our goal was not to exceed the existing mortgage payment but still have additional amenities in the house to make us happy. As a rule, the land will be approximately 20% of the property and additional equity in the house would help so that a larger home would not cost more per month, which was very interesting for us to find out. Our experience showed that we could own a home almost 50% larger than the existing one with about the same expenses per month.

Architecture

Once we had our plans, we had in-house help both for architecture and engineering. It was not a necessity, but it helped to get an idea of the cost and construction details. With civil and structural engineering background helped us make modifications in the design and construction. The drawings were modified in view of available information with newer technology and we wanted to exploit it to benefit us and possibly make a new beginning in the construction housing industry. Unfortunately, existing housing in this country has not made a great progress for a better housing. Early housing used to be well-built stone homes and later brick homes, but they became extinct and gave way to the abundant supply of cheaper wooden homes, which could be built faster and were much more profitable in business ventures. Today's home construction industry in the United States lacks innovation and vision for investment in our future. We in our house decided to become pioneers to build a home, which will be unique and therefore would set a standard for future homes. The house we were about to build, would not use wood as a primary material of construction. We thought of sustainability (as a loyal ASCE member) to keep as many of nature's resources as possible for future generations and the use of recycled materials and combine the commercial and residential technologies of construction. The external walls were made of insulated concrete forms (ICF) to give energy efficiency, while the inside walls used recycled steel (which is available) for the standard commercial walls to achieve speed and economy in construction. The floors were made of special "non-squeaking" composite concrete-steel, which are typically used in commercial construction, but modified to suit us. The construction was topped off with the use of the use of the natural resource of geothermal energy to give more energy efficiency. Although we could have added solar energy and other energy features, we did not due to personal factors in our experiment. In spite of all the unavoidable external hurdles, the overall result was very satisfying as the final product.

Construction

If you are constructing a home to a special design rather than using an already available set of plans, you may want to monitor the construction stage to some extent depending on your confidence level in the contractor. If you are managing the construction yourself you will need a written agreement with the contractor. In this case an attorney should be consulted. The major problems to be avoided are those that result in "extras," additional cost. Delays in scheduling are the most prominent difficulties that result in extra cost. Delays may occur because of man-made or natural (weather) conditions. Some are managed with vigilance and some are not. In certain regions, one should recognize that basement construction must be completed before the winter sets in or real problems may arise. Starting construction in late fall is problematic in northern latitudes.

Finishing Your Home

Finishing the home will depend on the individual owner's tastes, family requirements and the budget. Finishing with appurtenances, appliances, wall and floor coverings, etc, do not form part of the discussion of evaluating technologies used in the new home but are important. Finishing can be as simple or as elegant as desired. The furnishing stores (such as, electrical appliances, bathroom fixtures, etc) will design the systems for you and may give a good discount if you get their materials and equipment. In particular, the national chains,

Home Depot, Lowes, etc, can be very helpful during home building

One of the concerns the owner may have is whether the finished house will look any different than the conventional home. When the house is designed to an individual taste, built and enjoyed in that spirit, it will be a very marketable product. Not only the finished house presented here is similar to the conventional one, but will be much more likeable by anyone given the advantages of this home. In the authors' experience no one has mentioned any disadvantages.

Pictures During the Construction of the House

The cliché is true that a picture is worth a thousand words. There were lots of pictures and video, which were taken during the construction. The following section presents many pictures to give the reader a perspective of this project.

Picture 1 Site before construction. Site is cleared and ready for the work to begin.

GREEN HOUSE: THE ENERGY EFFICIENT HOME

Picture 2 Site before construction Note that as many trees as possible are saved in the backyard. Trees provide scenery, shade and cooler environment.

Picture 3 Basement level of construction; note that the level is much lower than the typical basement; this gives a good head room and a better living space for rooms in the basement.

Picture 4 Marking of outline for the house perimeter; the two white boards signify the width of footing for basement walls.

Picture 5 These ICF blocks are stacked at ground level. In the background, 3 layers of blocks are in place. Reinforcement helps when the soil is filled behind the cast-in-place concrete wall.

GREEN HOUSE: THE ENERGY EFFICIENT HOME

Picture 6 Partial wall forms are in place and ready to place the wall with ICF blocks. The large spiral shape pipe is for draining of water around the perimeter of the wall.

Picture 7 Pumping of concrete; pump helps economize the cost of wall by minimizing the labor. The wall can be built by 2-4 individuals maintaining the flow of concrete with light tapping on the forms to insure the concrete placement. Other person will insure the continuous supply of concrete in the pump.

GREEN HOUSE: THE ENERGY EFFICIENT HOME

Picture 8 Partially erected walls in the basement; note the height of ceiling for a better finished appearance. All vertical studs are made of recycled light-gage metal. They are available in different sizes with slots in place for running utility cables.

Picture 9 Shows partially completed basement. Although recycled steel studs for finishing, they are not necessary since the ICF blocks have embedded metal plates to attach the gypsum boards directly. These studs were placed at 24 inch spacing for easy finishing with 4 x 10 feet gypsum boards.

Picture 10 Floor is constructed with light-gage metal beams and metal deck with 1½" thick concrete. This replaces the conventional floor with no vibration or squeaking problem. The advantage is that the voids are already provided in the beams to receive pipes and maintain much better integrity and strength of the floor.

Picture 11 Metal deck is ready to receive concrete; its thickness is only 2 in. since the concrete acts in compression and is fully utilized. At the far end, the ICF blocks in place for the wall above are seen.

Picture 12 Interior walls are also built with recycled steel studs. Frames for each wall are conveniently made the same way as the wooden walls. The entire wall system is much lighter to handle. The bracing for the walls is provided before the next floor is placed.

Picture 13 Parts of exterior walls are also made with recycled studs where corners are not easy to finish.

Picture 14 Joint details of internal walls at the junction of two rooms. The frame can be conveniently erected to receive the next floor beams and the deck. Note the bracing and the floor beams with conventional spacing of 16 in.

Picture 15 shows the interior wall at the second floor level. Note the portion with recycled steel studs and opening ready for placing cables or wiring.

Picture 16 Shows economical use of recycled steel for construction of the staircase. The process was much simpler than buying the commercially available wooden staircases. With three staircases in the house, steel beams and studs were used efficiently. The 10 in. floor beams served as the treads, while the 6 in. studs worked as risers. It must be noted that the cost savings of 50% was achieved and the construction time was reduced.

Picture 17 In order to make sturdy staircase, the open web treads were filled with lean concrete. There was no strength requirement for the concrete but helped the rigidity in steps without any squeaking.

Picture 18 Staircase can be finished in any final form; wood finish was given to enhance the appearance of the entire foyer.

Picture 19 Next step in the construction is the roof and roof trusses. Due to the high pitch in the architecture, these light-gage steel trusses were made of two parts with 8 feet height and were assembled on ground with proper lateral supports for erection purpose.

GREEN HOUSE: THE ENERGY EFFICIENT HOME

Picture 20 Roof trusses were assembled on ground and erected using crane. The crane saved time and money and was extremely well suited for the job. The entire roof of almost 2,500 sq. ft. was erected in one morning.

Picture 21 shows partially completed roof and the garage portion of the roof. Part of the roof has to be built in place.

Picture 22 shows most of the completed roof; the exterior work for wall is being done along with the pilasters in the front. These are built as open (brick) column structures with central opening which was filled later with concrete for better rigidity. Part of the front wall was finished with stucco to enhance the aesthetics.

Picture 23 Energy source for the house is geothermal heat. The rig is ready to place 200 feet deep pipes to insure the required flow of liquid in the system. Both vertical and horizontal placement of pipes is possible, but they should be placed at least 3 feet below the grade level to take advantage of the constant temperature of earth below the frost line.

Picture 24: The rig is in full operation to drive the 20 ft sections in to the ground by connecting their ends. These pipes are driven by drop-hammer and are easily placed.

Picture 25: This picture shows connection between the two pipes.

Picture 26: Once the holes are drilled to the desired length, they are fitted with flexible PVC pipe, with U-shape at the bottom forming a closed loop system. Once they are placed, the steel casing pipes are withdrawn and the

cavity between the pipes and sides are filled with liquid Bentonite, which serves as heat conductor between the earth and the water in the pipes.

Picture 27: This picture shows the filling of the hole and the PVC pipe. This is then filled up with (glycol and) water for circulation for heating or cooling of the house.

Picture 28: The ends of these tubes are seen from the interior of the wall. Generally one tube is provided for 1,500 square feet of the finished space. They are connected on the second floor and at the basement level to have a 2-level HVAC system with conventional ductwork. These tubes are then

connected to the equipment in the house for heating and cooling. Once filled up with water and glycol, it will circulate without source.

Picture 29 shows partially finished walls with gypsum boards and the large patio glass door. All windows and doors were wood to match the décor of the house. The windows are swing types compared to the traditional sliding type.

Picture 30: Windows with elliptical tops provide elegant appearance. The finished walls are similar to the conventional house.

Picture 31: The large open kitchen and breakfast area are similar to the conventional home and are very pleasing with matching ceramic floor with black diamonds well-placed. The utility pipes are in-place, with part of the kitchen floor seen in the foreground.

Picture 32: Finished kitchen with appliances is typical of the large conventional homes.

Picture 33: The house is finished with brick exterior and electrical units for the front door and chandelier in foyer (partially seen).

Picture 34: Finished house with brick-finished garage side; the 3-car driveway is completed with concrete for durability compared to the conventional bituminous one.

GREEN HOUSE: THE ENERGY EFFICIENT HOME

Picture 35: The picture shows the beginning of the opening ceremony. It shows housewarming with ritual to thank the Almighty for his blessings and strength throughout the project to carry it to the end successfully.

Picture 36: The house as seen in the summer (2003)

Computer Application to Design Your Own Home

Introduction

So far in this book, information is presented on the innovative methods of using available materials to build a house. This information goes a long way toward allowing an individual to create that dream home and gain a sense of pride in one's own investment of time and resources. The house can be designed by an architect with information and ideas from the client/homeowner. With the recent explosion in technology, an individual with very little background in computers can design his/her own home and even furnish and decorate it on the screen. When complete, one can take a virtual tour of the house to ensure that the final product is exactly what is desired, as if one has visited the actual completed house.

Available computer software allows the user to see exactly what a dream home will look like in three dimensions. As a result, the user is able to criticize the design, examine the floor layout and furniture spacing, and a room may be made smaller or larger.

Why Design Your Own Home?

There is a great sense of pride and accomplishment that comes with designing a house based on one's own desires and dreams. The owner makes all the decisions, reviews them, approves them and finally, implements them. Many people today have ideas of a dream home tucked away in their heads. When the time comes to make this dream come true, or when there is sufficient capital, these people often turn to architectural expertise. Architects have the ability to put on paper in a professional manner what their clients have in mind. They may offer many types of typical home designs ranging from contemporary to traditional homes. Although this may be the case, the service of an architect can be quite costly and may put a strain on the available funds allocated for the project. With this in mind, it seems only reasonable that it may be a wise decision to design your own home. This can be easily done if one takes the time to get information about the software applicable for home design. With the advent of software such as Punch Home-Architect, a house can be easily designed quickly. Finally, designing one's own home can provide a high level of satisfaction and fulfillment.

Whether one is designing a simple home or a luxury estate, the process is the same and includes analytical thinking, creativity and visualization. The process also includes an honest communication with others: your spouse and children, your builder, and your banker. On the creative side, it means learning and taking the time to visualize the finished home from different angles, getting the "feel" of each room, including corners and hallways and gaining a sense of what it will be like to live in.

How To Do It And What Tools Are Available?

The process of designing starts with a vision. If one can imagine the finished dream home and has some idea of what components will satisfy the dream, the rest can come easily. One needs to get software that can bring the dream to reality. Currently, there are many programs available that can be used for the purpose of home design. However, not all of them are equally user friendly. If this is the case, one may get discouraged and frustrated. It is for this reason that programs such as the Punch! Super Home Suite and Chief Architect Home Edition were developed. The Punch! Software is a tool for creating one's own design. Little technical expertise is necessary. One can get familiarized with the functions by viewing the tutorial and/or by just starting to draw the ground/basement floor plan. You will have been on your way to designing your own home. This software is easily navigated due to the ease in which specific tools can be accessed, such as the wall or door "tool." Tools enable results to be seen within a few minutes of first using the software.

The process of designing a home will vary from one person to the next. The design process may or may not be limited by financial constraints, the location, and topography of the land, availability of building resources or preferences of the home-owner. Therefore, all constraints must be recognized, after which the overall design may be decided upon. If the lot area is a constraint, for example, then the house may be built higher instead of wider. The key house sections may then be addressed. Among others, these house sections include bedrooms bathrooms and living rooms. After assigning/locating these sections of the house the major part of the design is done.

Computer Programs for Designing Homes

Although only one design program is examined herein, there are several others and these are listed at the end of this Chapter. There are many programs/software on the market right now that afford the opportunity to create three dimensional designs. Some of these include DesignSoft, SmartDraw and as well as Punch! However for the purpose of these discussions we will concentrate on the punch software as it was tested and used by the Structures Class at Howard University for student class projects and was found to be user-friendly and simple to use.

Punch! Super Home Suite (Design Series)

This is a user friendly software application that allows the user to design a home in a fast and effective manner. The software is also fitted with a personal home estimator that records each element of the building as it is designed. A three dimensional viewing option as well as an interior view function is also available. It includes powerful tools, including CAD for 3D home and landscape design. You can plan your electrical and plumbing systems, design doors and windows, create custom trim, and much more.

Chief Architect Home Edition

This software is also user-friendly and allows individuals of all ages and educational backgrounds to prepare plans of a dream home. The "home edition" of the professional-grade software Chief Architect gives do-it-yourself home designers and remodelers drag-and-drop tools to create complex floor plan layouts, arrange rooms, insert customizable doors, windows, cabinets, fixtures, and furniture, generate several types of roofs automatically based on the layout of the floor beneath, and design landscaping.

Broderbund 3D Home Architect

Broderbund's 3D Home Design Suite lets you customize preset floor plans or create your own original. If one wants to see the vision of arched doorways leading out to the terrace, one can just point and click to create the shapes and lines as needed. Moldings and other details cab be selected from a menu of options, and coordinated with a group of rooms. A whole house can also be selected from a library. The other author, Martin, used this software to design his concrete home.

DesignWorkshop Lite

The DesignWorkshopLite software program lets one build 3-D models of architecture, landscapes, exhibits, or any kind of spatial design. While the software can be downloaded free, one can also order complete documentation, tutorials, and additional example building models for a small price.

Step-by-Step Approach to Designing a Home

The Punch! Super Home Suite program is a user-friendly program which allows even the most inexperienced user to design a home according to the user's desires and needs. On opening the program the user is shown a default screen which includes the table below:

1) **Menu Bar** –Used to carry out various commands
2) **Drawing Tools** – Used to develop various parts of house (walls, doors, etc.)
3) **Preview Bar** – Displays standard combinations of these parts
4) **Program Tools** – Used to control the working environment (move, rotate, etc.)
5) **Information Bar** – Gives information about a tool when mouse is over it
6) **Plan Window** – Surface on which house is constructed (Plan view)
7) **Menu Bar** –Used to carry out various commands
8) **Drawing Tools** – Used to develop various parts of house (walls, doors, etc.)
9) **Preview Bar** – Displays standard combinations of these parts
10) **Program Tools** – Used to control the working environment (move, rotate, etc.)
11) **Information Bar** – Gives information about a tool when mouse is over it
12) **Plan Window** – Surface on which house is constructed (Plan view)

Figure 0.1 Default Screen showing location of various tools

This is a brief overview of the location of the tools used in the program. A more detailed description is available in the Punch Home Suite User's Guide (*see chapters* 3-5). With this brief overview in mind, let us now use the various tools in the program to go through a step-by-step procedure for designing a home.

Start with your lot size and shape

The Lot Size (Ctrl+L) option allows you to define a "virtual lot" that more closely resembles your "physical lot."
First, from the Menu Bar click on:

Design → Lot Size...

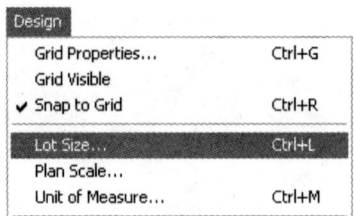

Enter the dimensions of your lot in feet or meters.

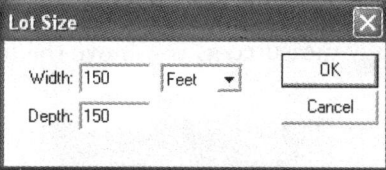

Tip: To draw a lot which is not rectangular (a cul de sac, for example) set the dimensions at your lot's largest point, then use the **CAD Tool** to draw the irregular edges.

Insert Walls

Exterior Walls
Now that the lot is defined, the next step is to outline the perimeter of your floor plan.

Click on the **Wall Tool**
Click on the **Walls** drop-down menu located at the top of the preview bar.

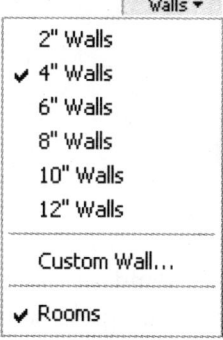

Select the appropriate wall thickness or if the desired thickness is not available in the list, select **Custom Wall...** and enter a custom thickness in inches.

GREEN HOUSE: THE ENERGY EFFICIENT HOME

Click on the Plan Window and drag the mouse to the desired length of the wall. You should see the length of the wall automatically measured as you move the mouse along the wall's path.

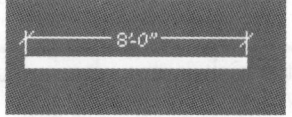

Repeat this step until you have outlined the perimeter of the floor plan.

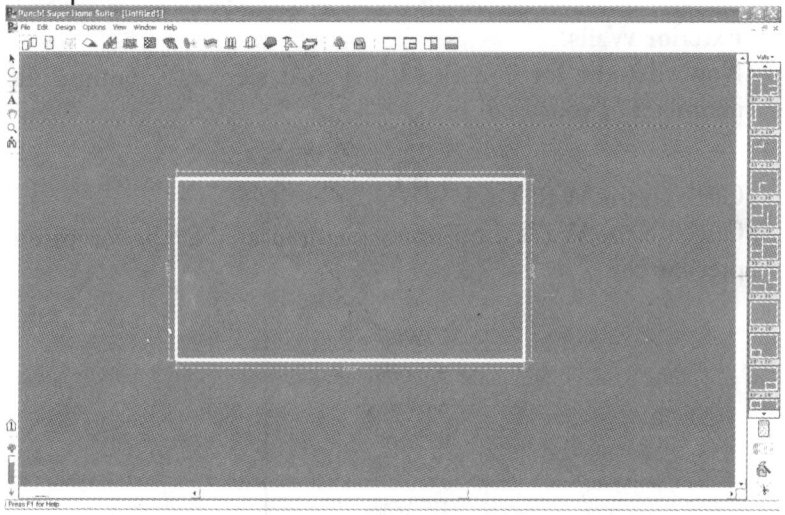

Tip: You may also select standard room patterns by dragging and dropping items from the preview bar on the right hand side of the screen unto the Plan Window.

Interior Walls
Select the Wall Tool again.
Draw in the interior walls to divide the floor plan into desired rooms:

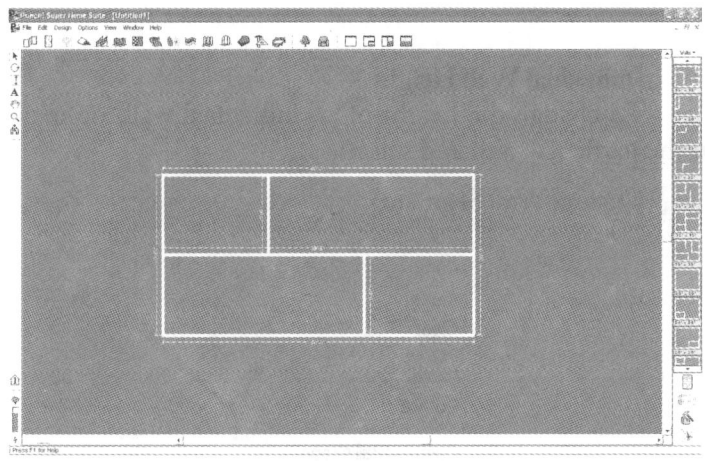

Change Wall Height and Thickness

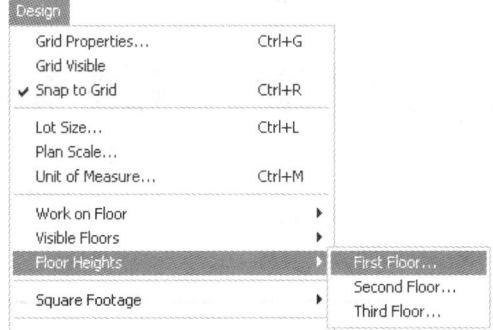

Floor Height (all walls)

You can now change the floor height of the entire first floor by clicking on:
Design → Floor Heights → First Floor

Enter the desired floor height in inches

Individual Wall Height

To change the height of an individual wall, right-click on the particular wall and select:

Custom Wall Segment...

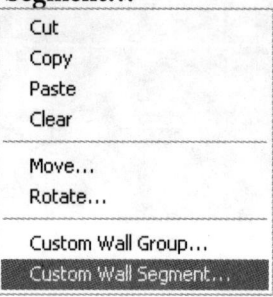

Enter the desired wall height in inches

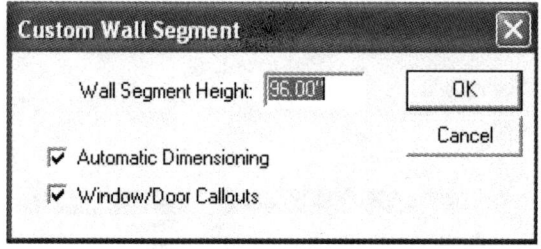

Individual Wall Thickness

To change the thickness of an individual wall, right-click on the particular wall and select:

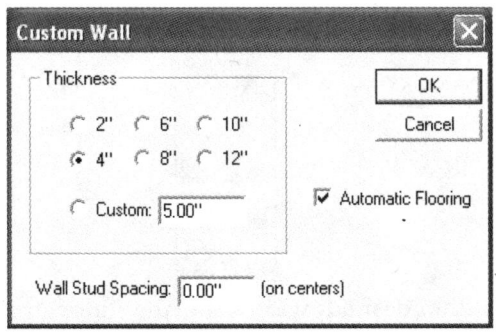

Custom Wall Group...

Select the desired thickness from the available choices or select **Custom** and enter it manually.
You can also alter the wall stud spacing for the wall.

Insert Doors & Openings

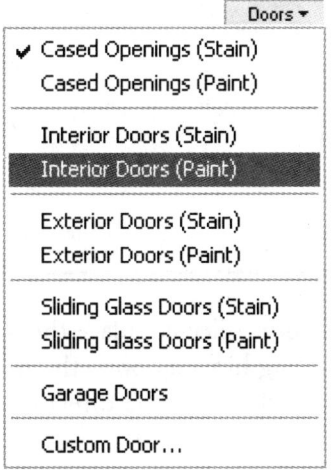

Select the **Door Tool**
Click on the **Doors** drop-down menu and select the appropriate door style. Choose **Interior Doors** for doors in between rooms and **Exterior Doors** for doors on an outside wall.

177

GREEN HOUSE: THE ENERGY EFFICIENT HOME

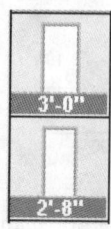

Click on the desired width for the door from the sizes available in the preview bar.

If the desired width is not available, click on **Custom Door...** from the **Doors** drop-down menu. Select the type of door and enter the desired dimensions.

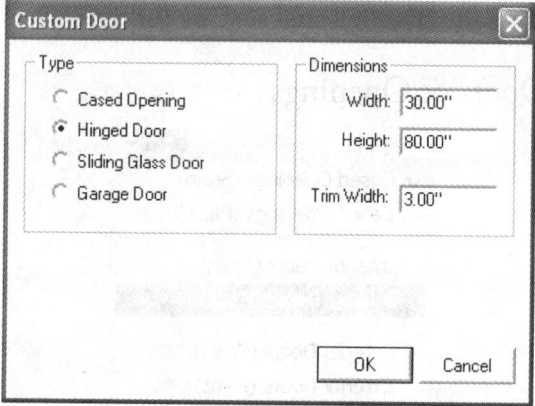

Once the type of door is selected, place the door in the desired location. When placing hinged doors, the first click places the door and the second click sets the direction and angle of the door.

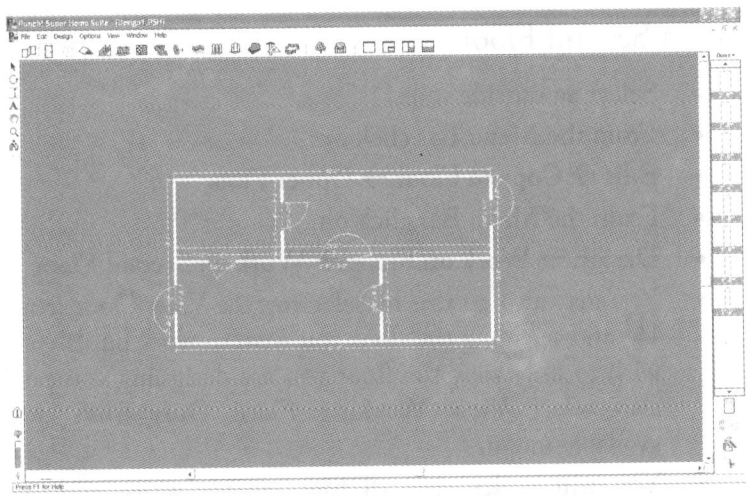

Insert Windows

Select the **Window Tool**

- Click on the Windows drop-down menu and select the appropriate window style. Choose the style (double hung or casement) and material (aluminum/vinyl or wood) for the desired window.
- Click on the desired dimensions for the window from the sizes available in the preview bar
- If the desired dimensions are not available in the preview bar, click on Custom Window... from the Windows drop-down menu. Enter the width, height, elevation, and trim width of the window.
- Once the type of window is selected, place the window in the desired location.

Tip: You may change the style of any window at any time by right-clicking on the window and selecting **Custom Window...** to enter the desired dimensions.

Tip: If you want to view your floor plan without dimensions, deselect **Automatic Dimensioning** and **Window/Door Callout** from the **Associative Dimension** icon at the bottom left hand corner of your window

GREEN HOUSE: THE ENERGY EFFICIENT HOME

Add a Second Floor

- Select an outside wall.
- From the Menu Bar click on:
- **Edit → Copy to Floor → Upper Floor**
- From the Menu Bar click on:
- **Design → Work on Floor → Work on Second Floor**
- You may also do this by selecting the **View Floor** icon and selecting the floor you wish to work on. If you wish to only view the floor you are designing you can also select **View Working Floor Only** from the available menu.
- You will notice that all four outside walls, and all doors and windows contained on these walls, were copied to the second floor. Delete the doors and windows you do not wish to retain.
- Design the second floor using the same tools used to design the first floor (walls, doors, and windows).

Draw Stairs & Railings

Draw Stairs

- Select the View Floor and Work On First Floor.
- Select the Stairs Tool
- The first click will set the beginning of the stairway and you will end them with a Right-click. You will be able to tell which way the stairs rise by the arrow.
- The next step is to create an opening on the second floor. Select the View Floor icon and Work On Second Floor.
- Select the Floor/Ground Covering Tool
- With a series of clicks define the opening.
- Select the Pointer Tool from the program tools on the right of your screen and Right-Click on the floor area.

180

- Select Floor Cut-Out from the Pop-up menu to convert the floor object to a floor cut-out.

Add a Railing
- Select the View Floor icon and Work On Second Floor.
- Select the Railing Tool
- With a series of clicks, define a railing around the opening you created in the previous step.

Add a Roof

- Select the View Floor icon and Work on Second Floor.
- Select the Roof Tool
- Select the style of roof desired from the choices available in the preview bar.
- Click on the Roofs drop-down menu and select the appropriate pitch. The pitch reflects the steepness of the roof (12:12 being the steepest and 4:12 the gentlest).
- If the desired pitch is not available in the preview bar, click on Custom Roof... from the Roofs drop-down menu. Select Custom and enter your desired pitch manually.
- Once the style of roof is selected, Drag and Drop your selection into the plan window.
- Move it into position by selecting the outside edge and resize it by selecting a corner.

Draw a Sidewalk

- Select the View Floor icon and Work On First Floor.
- Select the Pathway Tool

- Select the style of pathway desired from the choices available in the preview bar.
- Click on the Pathways drop-down menu and select the material and style of the pathway. Choose Sidewalks for any pedestrian walkways and Driveways for wider pathways designed for vehicles.
- With a series of clicks, define the sidewalk to the front door. End the sidewalk with a Right-click.
- You may change the shape of the pathway by moving the highlighted points which define the curve (if any) of the pathway.
- To change the width, double-click on any point on the pathway and enter the desired width in inches in the pop-up window.

Put in a Flowerbed and Edge It

- Select the Fill Tool
- From the preview bar, select the shape which most closely fits the desired fill. Drag and drop it into the plan window.
- To reshape it so that it conforms to the area's shape, select the individual points and move. them.
- Select the Edging Tool
- With a series of clicks, define the perimeter of the flowerbed. End the Edging with a Right-click.
- Select the Plants Tool
- From the Plants drop-down menu select the type of plant. Choose between Trees, Shrubs or Annuals.
- Drag and Drop the desired plants from the choices available in the preview bar into the flower bed, or anywhere else where a plant is desired.

Fence the backyard

- Select the Fence Tool
- From the Fencing drop-down menu select a type of fence.
- With a series of clicks define the perimeter of the area you want to fence. Double-click at the last point of the fence.
- Select the Gate Tool
- Drag and drop the desired gate from the preview bar into the fence in the plan window.

Tip: The gate will always conform to the fence style, if you define the fence as Privacy, the gate will follow suit.

Add a Deck

- Select the **Deck Tool**
- With a series of clicks, outline the area where you wish the deck to be.
- You may also Drag and Drop the deck from the choices available in the preview bar. Move it into position by selecting the outside edge and resize it by selecting a corner.
- Right-click on each deck section and specify whether you want that section to include railing, stairs, skirt trim, etc.

Add Colors and Textures

- Select the **3D Full View icon** from the top right of your window.
- Select the **Texture Tool**
- Click on the **Textures** drop-down menu and select the type of texture to be added to your outside walls.

GREEN HOUSE: THE ENERGY EFFICIENT HOME

- Drag & Drop the desired pattern from the Preview Bar onto each outer wall of your design. To expedite this process, Right-click on the texture from the preview bar then Right-click on each outer wall; end this process with a Double-click (left mouse button).
- Click on the **Textures** drop-down menu and select **Roofing**
- Drag & Drop your choice onto the roof.
- You may add textures to any surface by using this technique. Create textures for sidewalks, driveways, fill, or any other outdoor surface.
- Choose a texture for the floor interior and apply it. (Fabric/Carpet, Tile or Wood).
- Select the **Color Tool**
- Choose an appropriate color and Drag & Drop it onto the interior walls.

Tip: You're in no way limited to the **Colors** in the Preview Window. If you Double-click on any color you will be presented with the **Color Palette**. With this palette you are able to duplicate any color scheme you wish.

Add Objects

- Click on the **Split Plan View** icon
- Select the **Object Tool**
- Click on the **Objects** drop-down menu and select the type of object to be inserted.
- Drag & Drop the desired object from the Preview Bar onto the **Plan Window**. You should see the object displayed in the 3D View as you do this.
- Add as many objects as you like to the different rooms in your house. Move the objects around in the Plan Window until you are satisfied with how they look in the 3D View.

Examples of Worked-Out Designs

The design may be as simple or as complex as you wish. There are several options for using the software. You may wish to "sketch" your ideas to hand them to an architect for detailing. The software will allow you to prepare drawings in sufficient detail to engage a contractor. The greatest advantage of using design software is that many alternatives for room layout, size, orientation on a lot, and dozens of other aspects can be tested easily and at low cost, and the family can participate.

In this section a few examples of designs are presented. The first is by Dwight who has visions of a grand home with many added attractions including a swimming pool in the rear, not visible in this view. As quickly as pressing the button on the mouse, one can see the view from all four sides, separately.

The design below is by Mary who likes the exterior wall covering she selected and has spent some time on landscaping, as can be seen. Lighting on the large upper floor is enhanced by skylights. The three car garage will accommodate two cars and all the outdoor equipment she needs for maintaining the landscaping she plans to have.

GREEN HOUSE: THE ENERGY EFFICIENT HOME

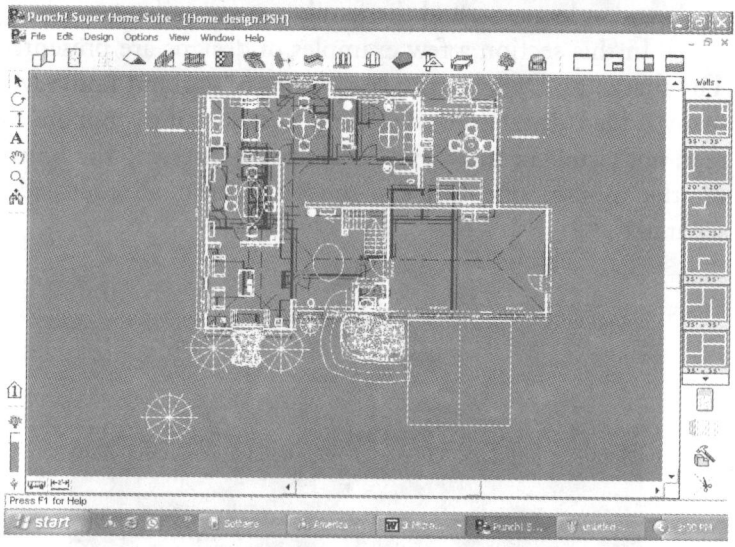

The Sabnis house from the next Chapter is shown below here with the basement beneath the house proper and one segment of the three car garage.

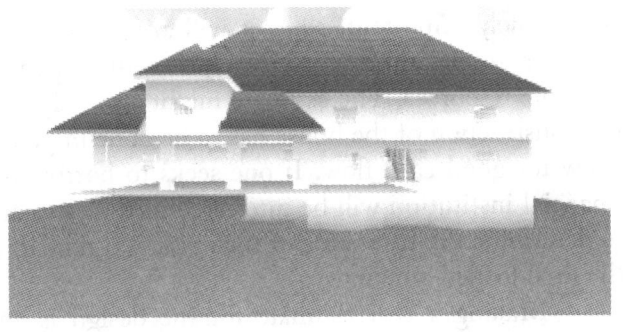

Virtually any view is possible using the software.

Below, another family was interested in seeing the possibilities for outdoor activity in their dream house. Even the dog put in his opinion for the location of his outside abode. This view reminded everyone that a door was needed in the vicinity to pass inside from the pool. A wet room just inside the door would be handy.

Estimating the Construction Cost

Why Bother Estimating?

The reality of the life is that everything comes down to "money." Thus, after one has conceived the dream house it must be determined if it is affordable. As such, a cost estimate is extremely important, since it will allow the owner (or the designer) to make the necessary adjustments depending on the available resources. The estimate might also help determine if the construction of the house has to be done in phases so as to allow for good cash flow. If one seeks to borrow money, the financial institution will be interested in the estimate in order to determine the true value of their risk and thus to determine the final loaned amount.

Making a cost estimate for the design is an essential part of the construction process. One will be able to examine the cost of the various elements of the design and choose between the various alternatives available based on the cost and the quality. Although cost is a major factor, the quality is also extremely important as the cheapest option is not always the best.

The estimate is needed in order to develop a suitable budget for construction as well as a budget and cash flow in the home-owner's affordable resources. Cost estimates are extremely important to the owner, the financing institution and the contractor. For the owner, cost estimate provides the basis for business decisions, including assessment of progress, development strategies and committing resources for further project development. For the others, the construction estimate is used to formulate execution strategies and provides a basis for construction planning.

Available Information

Information on estimating can be found in various construction estimating books and software. There are also many books which can be purchased that provide the current costing of both materials and labor. The measuring units for both would also be specified. A trusted name in this area is the *National Building Cost Manual Series*. The magazine Engineering News Record provides information on various construction materials and techniques, quarterly. These sources provide current material and labor prices in the construction industry. Information for cost estimates can also be obtained from the internet or a local library.

Some computer applications mentioned earlier, have an estimating section as part of the software. Punch! Super Home Suite is one such program; each element of the building is recorded as it is added by the user, and costs can be totaled at the end. References for construction quotes are available on www.get-a-quote.net. Quotes for materials can be obtained from the supply houses, such as Home Depot, Lowe's, and others.

Get Street-Smart With Your Project

The phrase "getting street smart" speaks to finding the most efficient and cost effective way to make your dream a reality. This of course starts with doing the design yourself, saving time and money. Then, by doing the estimate one can vary the cost of different grades and type of materials and fixtures in order to get the best value for money. The home owner should gain familiarity with terms and procedures used in the industry. This prevents the possibility of contractors or material suppliers taking advantage. Having a good knowledge of construction procedures will allow one to be familiar with the most effective construction methods and materials that can be applied to the project.

Benefits of Knowing Pitfalls

The major benefit of knowing possible pitfalls before hand is to save money. Mistakes cost money and time; if one can foresee possible problems, they can be avoided. Such pitfalls will come about as one goes through the design and estimating process. An initial idea may not seem to fit in well with the general scope of things or it may be found to be too expensive. This will prove to be a red flag in the general scope of things.

Pitfalls in construction estimating will most likely be due to desired features being accompanied by additional costs.

The most expensive areas in a home are usually the bathrooms and kitchen. The number of windows and the size and quality of windows can also affect the cost. Vaulted ceilings and high roof pitches can increase the cost of a home. When using other homes to calculate a comparison estimate, it must be ensured that the home has a similar style and features to that of the home that is being built.

The unit cost is often higher for a small home than a larger one. When building a larger home, the cost of expensive items (such as a furnace or kitchen) will be spread over more square footage. Also, it usually costs less to build a two-story home when compared to a one-story home that has the same square footage. This is because a two-story home will have a smaller roof and foundation. Plumbing and ventilation are more compact in two-story homes. Some details in the design of a home can make a big difference in the price. Some important factors to consider are:

- **Shape of the Home** - Homes that have a rectangular or box shape cost less to build. Having more angles and corners in the shape of your home can increase the amount of labor and materials needed to build a home. Dome shaped homes also make efficient use of materials and tends to cost less than other shapes.

- **Site Preparation** - Preparing a site for construction can have a big impact on the cost of a home. Building on a flat lot will usually cost less. If you have to haul in lots of dirt, do a lot of grading, clear trees, or blast through large rocks, then site preparations can become more expensive.

- **Inflation and Market Conditions** – Usually, the cost of building a home increases around 3% to 6% per year. Inflation must always be included if it will be several years before construction takes place. If other homes are used to compare prices, homes that have been built within the last six months should be used.

Summary - Designing a Home

The process of designing can be seen to be quite easy. It starts with an idea and it gradually evolves using the Punch! Software. The software proved to be user friendly with some limitation in design and estimating capabilities. It is ideal for the average home-owner who may convert his idea in to a real three-dimensional home. Designing a home with the help of the software available is quite simple and takes a limited amount of effort. Designing your own home can save you time as well as money. This fact is unknown to a large number of home owners. With this in mind, sharing this experience with others would be desirable to save your friends, family and associates thousands of dollars.

References

List of Some Available Software Programs

http://architecture.about.com/cs/cadprograms/tp/designsoftware.htm
http://www.punchsoftware.com/index.htm
http://www.download.com/3D-Home-Architect-Home-Design-Deluxe/
http://support.broderbund.com/
http://www.qualityplans.com/3dhome.htm
http://www.chiefarchitect.com/

GLOSSARY

Technical Terms

Insulated reinforced masonry system (IMSI)
Autoclaved aerated concrete (AAC)
Expanded polystyrene (EPS)
Structural insulated panels (SIP)
Exterior insulation and finish systems (EIFS)
Extruded polystyrene (XPS)
Insulating concrete forms (ICF)

Rebar -- reinforcing steel bars

Batt -- means pre-cut pieces of insulation material (such as, fiberglass, recycled cotton etc.), often in a packet.

R-value – a measure of the capability of a material to resist heat flow. A high value means high resistance. In this book, steady state R-values are presented exclusively.

Mass-enhanced R-values (usually called "effective R-values") are never used.

Thermal mass - a "term of art" that at present has no technical definition. The sense is that a high mass material such as concrete has a greater impact on modulating heat flow than a low mass material. An excellent, understandable technical discussion can be found at http://www.buildinggreen.com/auth/article.cfm?fileName=070401a.xml

HVAC -- heating, ventilating and air conditioning

ft^2 or sq ft – square foot

psi – lb/sq in -- pounds per square foot

in. -- inch

lbs/ft^3 or lb/cu ft -- pounds per cubic foot, a measure of density

Photovoltaic (PV) technology
Ethylene vinyl acetate (EVA) – a component of a solar cell.
Kilowatt peak (kWp)
Whole Building Design (WBD)

Organizations and Other Terms

Pre-cast and Pre-stressed Concrete Institute (PCI)
The Portland Cement Association (PCA)
National Association of Home Builders (NAHB)
Insulated Concrete Forms Association (ICFA)
Department of Housing and Urban Development (HUD)
American Cement Corporation (ACC)
Portland Cement Institute (PCI)
American Concrete Institute (ACI)
National Association of Home Builders Research Center (NAHBRC)
US Department of Energy (DOE)
DOEs Energy Efficiency and Renewable Energy (EERE's) Building Technologies Program
US Environmental Protection Agency (EPA)
National Science Foundation (NSF)
National Ready Mix Concrete Association (NRMCA)
Energy-efficient mortgage (EEM)
National Home Energy Rating Systems Council (NHERSC)
Residential Energy Services Network (RESN)
Home Energy Rating System (HERS)
U.S. Department of Veterans Affairs (VA)
Federal Housing Authority (FHA)